SOCIAL INFLUENCE

ROB MCILVEEN & RICHARD GROSS

Hodder & Stoughton

A MEMBER OF THE HODDER HEADLINE GROUP

Dedication

To all students of Psychology: past, present and future

British Library Cataloguing in Publication Data
A catalogue record for this title is available from the British Library

ISBN 0 340 74900 8

First published 1999
Impression number   10 9 8 7 6 5 4 3 2 1
Year   2003 2002 2001 2000 1999

Typeset by GreenGate Publishing Services, Tonbridge, Kent.
Printed and bound in Great Britain for Hodder and Stoughton Educational, a division of Hodder Headline plc, 338 Euston Road, London NW1 3BH, by Cox & Wyman, Reading, Berks

CONTENTS

The *Aspects of Psychology* series aims to provide a short and concise, but detailed and highly accessible, account of selected areas of psychological theory and research.

Social Influence consists of four chapters. Chapter 1 discusses conformity, Chapter 2 obedience, and Chapter 3 leadership. Chapter 4 is concerned with collective behaviour.

For the purposes of revision, we have included detailed summaries of the material presented in each chapter. Instead of a separate glossary, for easy reference the Index contains page numbers in **bold** which refer to definitions and main explanations of particular concepts.

ACKNOWLEDGEMENTS

We would like to thank Dave Mackin, Anna Churchman and Denise Stewart at GreenGate Publishing for their swift and efficient preparation of the text. Thanks also to Greig Aitken at Hodder for all his hard work in coordinating this project (we hope it's the first of many!), and to Tim Gregson-Williams for his usual help and support.

Picture Credits

The publishers would like to thank the following for permission to reproduce photographs and other illustrations in this book:

p.1 (Fig 1.1), Private Eye; p.22 (Fig 2.1),Pinter & Martin Ltd, HarperCollins Publishers, Inc., New York; p.24 & p.26 (Figs 2.2, 2.3), from the film *Obedience*, copyright © 1965 by Stanley Milgram and distributed by Penn State Media Sales; p.28 (Fig 2.4), from *Psychology* by Zimbardo P.G. & Weber A.L. (1994), copyright © 1994 by Philip G. Zimbardo and Ann L. Weber. Reprinted by permission of Addison-Wesley Educational Publishers Inc; p.56 (Fig 3.2), AKG photo London; p.62 (Fig 4.1), Camera Press Ltd; p.68 (Fig 4.2), Corbis-Bettman; p.70 (Fig 4.3), Prentice-Dunn, S. & Rogers, R.W. (1983) *Journal of Personality and Social Psychology*, 8, 377–383. Copyright © 1968 by the American Psychological Association. Reprinted with permission.

The publisher would also like to thank the following for permission to reproduce text extracts: p.65 (Box 4.4), from *Race Riot* by A.M. Lee and N.D. Humphrey, copyright © 1943 by A.M. Lee and N.D. Humphrey. Reprinted by permission of Henry Holt & Company, Inc.

Every effort has been made to obtain necessary permission with reference to copyright material. The publishers apologise if inadvertently any sources remain unacknowledged and will be glad to make the necessary arrangements at the earliest opportunity.

CONFORMITY

Introduction and overview

Conformity has been defined in a number of ways. For Crutchfield (1955), it is 'yielding to group pressure', whilst Mann (1969) argues that whereas this is its essence, 'it may take different forms and be based on motives other than group pressure'. Zimbardo & Leippe (1991) see conformity as:

> 'a change in belief or behaviour in response to real or imagined group pressure when there is no direct request to comply with the group nor any reason to justify the behaviour change'.

What the definitions above have in common is that they all make reference to *group pressure*, although none of them specifies particular groups with particular beliefs or practices. Rather, it is the pressure exerted by *any* group which is important to a person at a given time that is influential. These may be composed of 'significant others' such as family or peers (*membership groups*), or groups whose values a person admires or aspires to, but is not actually a member of (*reference groups*). Conformity, then, does not imply adhering to any particular set of attitudes or values. Instead, it involves yielding to the real or imagined pressures of *any* group regardless of its majority or minority status (van Avermaet, 1996).

Experimental research into conformity began in the early 1930s, and the phenomenon continues to attract research interest today. This chapter reviews what is known about conformity to real or imagined pressure from others.

Figure 1.1 *A humorous look at conformity*

Experimental studies of conformity

Sherif (1935) had participants make estimates of the amount by which a spot of light in an otherwise darkened room appeared to move (the *autokinetic effect*). In one experiment, participants first made their estimates privately and then as members of a group. Sherif found that participants' individual estimates converged, and became more alike. Thus, a *group norm* developed which represented the average of the individual estimates (see Figure 1.3, page 3).

Whilst Sherif believed that his study demonstrated conformity, Asch (1951) disagreed. According to Asch, the fact that Sherif's task was ambiguous, in that there was no right or wrong answer, made it difficult to draw conclusions about conformity in group situations. In Asch's view, the best way to measure conformity was in terms of a person's tendency to agree with other people who unanimously give the *wrong answer* on a task with an obvious and unambiguous solution. Asch devised a simple perceptual task that involved participants deciding which of three comparison lines of varying length matched a standard line.

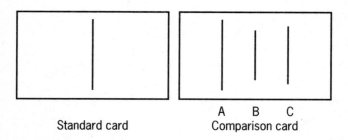

Standard card   A   B   C
                 Comparison card

Figure 1.2   *An example of the line-judgement task devised by Asch*

In a pilot study, Asch tested 36 participants individually on 20 slightly different versions of the task shown in Figure 1.2. Since they made a total of only three mistakes in the 720 trials (an error rate of 0.42 per cent), Asch concluded that the tasks were

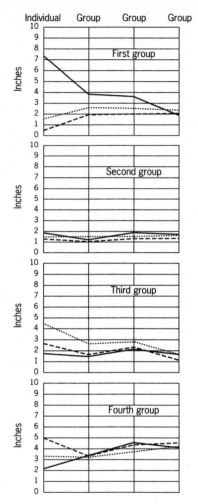

Figure 1.3 *Median judgements of the apparent movement of a stationary point of light given by participants in Sherif's (1935) experiment. In the data shown, participants first made their estimates alone ('individual') and then in groups of three on three occasions ('group'). The figure shows the estimates given by four groups. Sherif also found that when the procedure was reversed, that is, participants made three estimates in groups followed by an estimate alone, the 'individual' estimates did not deviate from one another (From Sherif, 1936)*

simple and their answers obvious and unambiguous. Asch's procedure for studying conformity was ingenious and, because the
basic set-up can be adapted to investigate the effects of different
variables on conformity, it is known as the *Asch paradigm*.

Box 1.1   *The Asch paradigm*

Some of the participants who had taken part in Asch's pilot study
(see text) were requested to act as 'stooges' (or confederates). The
stooges were told that they would be doing the tasks again, but
this time in a *group* rather than individually. They were also told
that the group would contain one person who was completely
ignorant that they were stooges.

On certain *critical* trials, which Asch would indicate by means of a
secret signal, all the stooges were required to say *out loud* the same
wrong answer. In Asch's original experiment, the stooges (usually
seven to nine of them) and the naïve participant were seated either
in a straight line or round a table (see Figure 1.4) The situation was
rigged so that the naïve participant was always the last or last but
one to say the answer out loud.

On the first two trials, all the stooges gave the correct answers.
However, on the third trial they unanimously gave a wrong answer.
In all, this happened a further 11 times in the experiment, with four
additional 'neutral' trials (in which all stooges responded with the
correct answers) between the critical trials.

The important measurement in the Asch paradigm is whether
the naïve participant conforms and gives the same wrong answer
as the stooges have unanimously done, or is independent and
gives the obviously correct answer.

Asch found a *mean* conformity rate of 32 per cent, that is,
participants agreed with the incorrect majority answer on about
one third of the critical trials. If the *median* is used as the measure of central tendency, the conformity rate is 25 per cent.
However, and as Table 1.1 shows, there are wide individual differences. Thus, no one conformed on all the critical trials, and
13 of the 50 participants tested (26 per cent) never conformed
at all. However, one person conformed on 11 of the 12 critical

Figure 1.4   *A naïve participant (number 6), having heard five stooges give the same incorrect answer, offers his own judgement as to which of three comparison lines matches a stimulus line*

Table 1.1 *The findings from Asch's original experiment*

No. of conforming responses made	No. of people making those responses
0	13
1	4
2	5
3	6
4	3
5	4
6	1
7	2
8	5
9	3
10	3
11	1
12	0

trials and about three-quarters conformed at least once. Given that the task was simple and unambiguous, such findings indicate a high level of conformity. As van Avermaet (1996) has remarked:

> 'the results reveal the tremendous impact of an "obviously" incorrect but unanimous majority on the judgements of a lone individual'.

How did the naïve participants explain their behaviour?

After the experiment, participants were interviewed about their behaviour. The interviews revealed a number of specific reasons for the occurrence of conformity. For example, some participants claimed that they wanted to act in accordance with what they imagined were the experimenter's wishes, and convey a favourable impression of themselves by 'not upsetting the experiment' (which they believed they would have done by disagreeing with the majority).

Others, who had no reason to believe that there was anything wrong with their eyesight, claimed they genuinely doubted the validity of their own judgements by wondering if they were suffering from eye strain, or if the chairs had been moved so that they could not see the task material properly. Yet others denied being aware of having given incorrect answers – they had unwittingly used the stooges as 'marker posts' (Smith, 1995). Some participants said that they 'didn't want to appear different', or 'didn't want to be made to look a fool' or 'inferior'. For them, there was clearly a discrepancy between the answer they gave in the group and what they *privately believed*. Whilst they knew the answer they were giving was wrong, they nonetheless went along with the views of the group (see page 14).

That participants were justified in fearing potential ridicule by group members was shown in an experiment in which 16 naïve participants and a *single stooge* were tested (van Avermaet, 1996). When the stooge gave a wrong answer on the critical trials, the naïve participants reacted with sarcasm and laughter. In other experiments, Asch (1952) showed that when the stooges gave their answers out loud, but the naïve participant *wrote down* the answers, conformity was significantly reduced. This indicates that it must have been *group pressure*, rather than anything else, that produced conformity.

There is evidence to suggest that participants in Asch-type experiments experience some degree of *stress*. For example, Bogdonoff *et al.* (1961) showed that plasma-free fatty acid levels (a measure of arousal) increased in naïve participants as they heard the stooges giving wrong answers. When the naïve participant responded, the levels decreased if a conforming response was made, but continued to increase if a non-conforming response was given.

Factors affecting conformity

Using the Asch paradigm, researchers have, as noted earlier, manipulated particular variables in order to see if they increase or decrease the amount of conformity reported in Asch's original experiment.

Box 1.2 *Some factors affecting conformity*

Group size: With one stooge and the naïve participant, conformity is very low (3 per cent), presumably because it is a simple case of the participant's 'word' against the stooge's. With two stooges, conformity rises to 14 per cent. With three stooges, it reaches the 32 per cent which Asch originally reported. Thereafter, however, further increases in group size do not lead to increases in conformity. With very large groups, conformity may drop dramatically (Asch, 1955), one reason being that participants begin (quite rightly) to suspect collusion (Wilder, 1977).

Unanimity: Conformity is most likely to occur when the stooges are unanimous in their answers. When one stooge does not go along with the majority judgement, conformity decreases (Asch, 1956). The stooge need not even share the naïve participant's judgement (the stooge may, for example, appear to have a visual impairment as evidenced by the wearing of thick glasses). Thus, just breaking the unanimity of the majority is sufficient to reduce conformity (Allen &

Levine, 1971). For Asch, unanimity is a more important factor than group size:

> 'a unanimous majority of three is, under given conditions, far more effective (in producing conformity) than a majority of eight containing one dissenter' (Asch, 1951).

Additionally, when a stooge begins by giving the correct answer but then conforms to the majority incorrect answer, conformity is increased.

Task difficulty, ambiguity, and familiarity with task demands: With difficult tasks, as when the comparison lines are all similar to the stimulus line, conformity increases (Asch, 1956). Ambiguous tasks, such as making judgements about the number of clicks produced by a fast metronome, also produce increased conformity (Shaw *et al.*, 1957). The more familiar we are with a task's demands, the less likely we are to conform. For example, women are more likely to conform to group pressure on tasks involving the identification of tools (such as wrenches), whereas men are more likely to conform on tasks involving the identification of cooking utensils (Sistrunk & McDavid, 1971).

Gender and other individual differences: It has been reported that women conform more than men (Cooper, 1979), although this claim has been disputed. For example, Eagly & Steffen (1984) found that men conform to group opinions as frequently as women do when their conformity or independence will be kept private. However, when conformity or independence will be made known to the group, men conform less than women, presumably because nonconformity is consistent with the masculine stereotype of independence. Conformity has also been found to be higher amongst those who:

- have low self-esteem (Santee & Maslach, 1982);
- are especially concerned about social relationships (Mullen, 1983);
- have a strong need for social approval (Sears *et al.*, 1991);
- are attracted towards other group members (Wyer, 1966).

Evaluating Asch's contribution to the study of conformity

One of the earliest criticisms of Asch's work was that the Asch paradigm was both time consuming (in terms of setting up the situation) and uneconomical (in the sense that only one naïve participant at a time can be investigated). Crutchfield (1954) attempted to overcome both of these problems.

Box 1.3   *Crutchfield's procedure*

In Crutchfield's procedure, participants are seated in a cubicle which has a panel with an array of lights and switches (the *Crutchfield device*). Questions can be projected on to a wall and, by pressing switches, the participant can answer them. The participant is told that the lights on the panel represent the responses given by other participants. In fact, this is not true, and the lights are controlled by an experimenter who has a 'master panel' in another cubicle.

Of course, the participant does not know this, and the arrangement removes the need for stooges. It also allows several participants in different cubicles to be tested at once. Crutchfield tested over 600 people.

Amongst many findings were those indicating that college students agreed with statements which, in other circumstances, they would probably not agree with. These included statements like 'The life expectancy of American males is only 25 years', 'Americans sleep four to five hours per night and eat six meals a day' and 'Free speech being a privilege rather than a right, it is only proper for a society to suspend free speech when it feels itself threatened'.

Asch's original findings have stimulated much research. Twenty or so years after they were published, Larsen (1974) found significantly lower rates of conformity among American students. Larsen explained the discrepancy in terms of a change in climate of opinion in America:

'away from the stupefying effects of McCarthyism in the 1950s [towards] a more sceptical and independent individual'.

Five years later, however, Larsen *et al.* (1979) found conformity rates similar to those reported by Asch, possibly suggesting a move *away* from independence and criticism in American students.

In Britain, Perrin & Spencer (1981) found very low rates of conformity among university students. However, when they tested young offenders on probation, with probation officers as stooges, very similar rates of conformity to those reported by Asch were obtained. According to Perrin and Spencer, the rate of conformity obtained in studies is a useful indicator of the cultural expectations people bring to the experiment from their contemporary world, a view with which Asch agreed (Perrin & Spencer, 1980). However, as well as participants' expectations influencing the amount of conformity obtained, it is possible that *experimenters* exert an influence too. As Brown (1985) has noted, experimenters may also have changed over time. Perhaps their expectations of the amount of conformity that will occur in an experiment are unwittingly conveyed to the participants, who respond accordingly.

Majority or minority influence in Asch-type experiments?

In reviewing the findings from Asch's studies, Turner (1991) observed that most concern has centred around:

> **'the weakness of the individual in face of the group and the strength of spontaneous pressures for conformity inherent in the group context'.**

However, and as Table 1.1 shows (see page 5), most participants remained independent either most or all of the time, and so conformity was actually the *exception* to the rule.

Typically, the stooges in an Asch-type experiment are thought of as the majority and, numerically, they are. However, Moscovici & Faucheux (1972) have argued that it is more profitable to think of the naïve participant as the majority (in that he or she embodies the 'conventional', self-evident opinion of most of us) and the stooges as the minority (who reflect an unorthodox, unconventional, eccentric and even outrageous viewpoint). In Asch's experiments, this minority influenced the majority 32 per cent of the time, and it is those participants remaining independent who are actually the conformists!

Asch-type experiments, viewed from this perspective, offer evidence related to the question of how new ideas come to be accepted, rather than about the processes that operate to maintain the *status quo* (Tanford & Penrod, 1984). In Moscovici's (1976) view, a *conformity bias* exists in this area of research, such that all social influence serves the need to adapt to the *status quo* for the sake of uniformity and stability. However, change is sometimes needed to adapt to changing circumstances, and this is very difficult to explain given the presence of a conformity bias. What is needed is an understanding of the dynamics of *active minorities*. If such minorities did not exert influence in any arena of human social and scientific activity, innovations would simply never happen (van Avermaet, 1996).

How do minorities exert an influence?

If the data from Asch's original experiments are reanalysed, conformity or non-conformity can be shown to be related to the *consistency* of the stooge's judgements (Moscovici, 1976). Moscovici and his colleagues were able to show that by giving consistent responses, minorities can change the majority's views. In one experiment, Moscovici & Lage (1976) instructed a stooge minority of two to consistently describe a blue-green colour as green. The majority's views changed to that of the minority, and this effect persisted when further judgements were asked for after the minority had withdrawn from the experiment.

Box 1.4 *Why are consistency and other factors important in minority influence?*

According to Hogg & Vaughan (1995), consistency has five main effects:
1 It disrupts the majority norm, and produces uncertainty and doubt.
2 It draws attention to itself as an entity.
3 It conveys the existence of an alternative, coherent point of view.

> **4** It demonstrates certainty and an unshakeable commitment to a particular point of view.
>
> **5** It shows that the only solution to the current conflict is the minority viewpoint.
>
> Minorities are also more effective if they are seen to have made significant personal/material sacrifices (*investment*), are perceived as acting out of principle rather than ulterior motives (*autonomy*), and display a balance between being 'dogmatic' (*rigidity*) and 'inconsistent' (*flexibility*) (Nemeth & Wachtler, 1973; Papastamou, 1979; Wood *et al.*, 1994; Hogg & Vaughan, 1995). Minorities also have more influence if they are seen as being similar to the majority in terms of age, gender and social category (Clark & Maass, 1988), and particularly if minority members are categorised as part of the ingroup.

Why do people conform?

As Abrams *et al.* (1990) have noted:

> 'we know groups constrain and direct the actions of their members, but there is considerable controversy as to how, and under what conditions, various forms of influence operate'.

One attempt to account for conformity was provided by Deutsch & Gerard (1955). They argued that in order to explain group influence, it was necessary to distinguish between *informational social influence* (ISI) and *normative social influence* (NSI).

Informational social influence

Festinger's (1954) *social comparison theory* states that people have a basic need to evaluate ideas and attitudes and, in turn, to confirm that these are correct. This can provide a reassuring sense of control over the world and a satisfying sense of competence. In situations which are novel or ambiguous, social reality is defined by the thoughts and behaviours of others. For example, if we are in a restaurant and not clear about which piece of cutlery to use with a particular course, we look to others for 'guidance' and then conform to their behaviours. This is ISI.

The less we can rely on our own direct perceptions and behavioural contacts with the physical world, the more susceptible we should be to influences from other people (Turner, 1991). As mentioned earlier (see page 6), some participants in Asch's experiment claimed that they believed the majority opinion to be correct and that their own perceptions were incorrect. Taken at face value, this would suggest that ISI occurs even in unambiguous situations (Insko *et al.*, 1983). However, such explanations may actually be *defensive* (or perhaps *self-serving*) *attributions* given by participants to justify submission to the influence of the majority (Berkowitz, 1986).

Normative social influence

Underlying NSI is the need to be accepted by others and to make a favourable impression on them. We may conform in order to gain social approval and avoid rejection, and we may agree with others because of their power to reward, punish, accept, or reject us. As noted previously, in both Asch's and Crutchfield's experiments, most participants were quite clear as to the correct answer. However, in making their own judgements they risked rejection by the majority, and so for at least some participants conformity probably occurred because of NSI.

Box 1.5 *The costs of non-conformity*

Schachter (1951) provided evidence that the fear that others will reject, dislike or mistreat us for holding different opinions is justified. Groups of male university students read and discussed the case of a delinquent youth called 'Johnny Rocco'. Johnny was described as having grown up in an urban slum, experiencing a difficult childhood, and having often been in trouble. Participants were asked to recommend that Johnny receive a great deal of love and affection, harsh discipline and punishment, or some combination of the two.

Johnny's case notes were written sympathetically, and participants made lenient recommendations. Included in each group, however, was a stooge who sometimes agreed with the genuine participants and sometimes recommended that Johnny be given harsh discipline and punishment. When the stooge adopted the deviant opinion, he maintained and defended it as best he could.

Schachter found that participants immediately directed their comments to the stooge in an effort to get him to agree with their lenient recommendations. When the stooge failed to do this, communication dropped off sharply and he was largely ignored. After the discussion, participants were asked to assign group members to various tasks and recommend who should be included in the group. When the stooge's opinion deviated from the group majority, he was rejected. However, in groups where he took the majority opinion, he was viewed positively and not rejected.

So, holding an unpopular opinion, even in a short group discussion, can lead to an individual being ostracised, and it seems reasonable to suggest that under at least some circumstances, a fear of rejection for failing to conform is justified.

Internalisation and compliance

Related to NSI and ISI are two major *kinds* of conformity. *Internalisation* occurs when a private belief or opinion becomes consistent with a public belief or opinion. In internalisation, then, we say what we believe and believe what we say. Mann (1969) calls this *true conformity*, and it can be thought of as a conversion to other people's points of view. This probably explains the behaviour of participants in Sherif's experiment (see page 2). In Asch-type conformity experiments, however, people face conflicts and reach compromises in the form of *compliance*, in which the answers given publicly are *not* those that are privately believed. In compliance, then, we say what we do not believe and what we believe we do not say.

Conformity and group belongingness

The distinction between NSI and ISI has been called the *dual process dependency model of social influence*. However, this model underestimates the role of group 'belongingness'. One important feature of conformity is that we are influenced by a group because, psychologically, we feel we belong to it. This is why a group's norms are relevant standards for our own attitudes and behaviour. The dual process dependency model emphasises the *interpersonal* aspects of conformity experiments, which could just as easily occur between individuals as group members.

> **Box 1.6**   *Referent social influence*
>
> Abrams *et al.* (1990) argue that we only experience uncertainty when we disagree with those with whom we expect to agree. This is especially likely when we regard those others as members of the same category or group as ourselves in respect to judgements made in a shared stimulus situation. Social influence occurs, then, when we see ourselves as belonging to a group and possessing the same characteristics and reactions as other group members. Turner (1991) calls this self-categorisation in which group membership is salient *referent informational influence.*

Abrams *et al.*'s approach suggests that in Sherif's (1935) experiment, for example, participants were influenced by the assumption that the autokinetic effect is actually real, and their expectations of agreement between themselves. In support of this, it has been shown that when participants discover that the autokinetic effect is an illusion, mutual influence and convergence cease because the need to agree at all is removed (Sperling, 1946).

If, however, we believe that there is a correct answer, and we are uncertain what it is, *only* those whom we categorise as belonging to 'our' group will influence our judgements. As Brown (1988) has remarked:

> 'there is more to conformity than simply "defining social reality": it all depends on who is doing the defining'.

According to this self-categorisation approach, people conform because they are group members, and evidence indicates that conformity on Asch-type experiments is higher when participants see themselves as ingroup members (Abrams *et al.*, 1990).

This implies that it is not the validation of physical reality or the avoidance of social disapproval that is important. Rather, it is the upholding of a group norm that is important, and *people* are the source of information about the appropriate ingroup norm.

Conformity: good or bad?

Sometimes, *dissent* is just an expression of disagreement, a refusal to 'go along with the crowd'. On other occasions, it is more creative, as when someone suggests a better solution to a problem (Maslach *et al.*, 1985). A refusal to 'go along with the crowd' may be an attempt to remain independent as a matter of principle (which Willis, 1963, calls *anticonformity*) and may betray a basic fear of a loss of personal identity. Constructive dissent and independence, by contrast, are positive qualities.

In most circumstances, conformity serves a valuable social purpose in that it:

'lubricates the machinery of social interaction [and] enables us to structure our social behaviour and predict the reactions of others' (Zimbardo & Leippe, 1991).

For most people, though, the word 'conformity' has a negative connotation and is often used to convey undesirable behaviour. In laboratory research, conformity has most often been studied in terms of 'the conspiratorial group' who 'limit, constrain, and distort the individual's response' (Milgram, 1965).

As a result, it has been implicitly assumed that independence is 'good' and conformity is 'bad', a value judgement made explicit by Asch (1952). However, conformity can be highly functional, helping us satisfy social and non-social needs, as well as being necessary (at least to a degree) for social life to proceed at all. Moreover, because each of us has a limited (and often biased) store of information on which to make our decisions, why shouldn't we consider information from others, especially those with more expertise than us? A conforming response, then, may be a *rational judgement* by a person who does not have sufficient information on which to make a decision, and so relies on others for assistance. However, whilst dissent can create unpleasantness, and conformity can help preserve harmony:

> 'there are obvious dangers to conformity. Failure to speak our minds against dangerous trends or attitudes (for example, racism) can easily be interpreted as support' (Krebs & Blackman, 1988).

Conclusions

There are some circumstances in which we conform as a result of either real or imagined pressure from others. Exactly why we sometimes conform and sometimes show independent behaviour has been the subject of much research, and many factors influencing conformity have been identified. Whilst conformity is usually viewed as the influence of a majority over a minority, minorities can, under certain circumstances, exert influence over majorities.

Summary

- The essence of conformity is yielding to real or imagined **group** (**membership** or **reference**) **pressure** in the absence of any direct request to comply with the group. Conformity does not imply adhering to particular attitudes or values, and the group may have majority or minority status.
- The **Asch paradigm** enables conformity to be studied experimentally. In this, a naïve participant is led to believe that other participants ('stooges') are genuine when in fact they are not. The 'stooges' sometimes unanimously give incorrect answers on a task which has an obviously correct answer. The crucial measurement is whether the naïve participant gives the same wrong answer as the 'stooges' on critical trials.
- Asch found a mean conformity rate of 32 per cent (or 25 per cent if the median is used). No participant conformed all the time, but all conformed at least once in Asch's original experiment. Participants explained their behaviour in several ways.

Some wondered if their eyesight was reliable, or said they conformed because they did not want to look foolish. Others denied being aware they had given incorrect answers.

- When naïve participants are allowed to write down their answers, conformity disappears, indicating that **group pressure** is the critical factor. Increases in participants' physiological arousal indicates that the Asch paradigm is a stressful experience.

- Several factors influence the amount of conformity observed when the Asch paradigm is used. These include **group size**, **unanimity**, **task difficulty**, **ambiguity**, and **familiarity**. **Gender** and other individual differences can also influence how much conformity occurs.

- A less time-consuming and more economical way of studying conformity is provided by the **Crutchfield device**. This produced similar amounts of conformity to those originally reported by Asch.

- The amount of conformity observed in American students has not remained constant over time. In Britain, low rates of conformity have been reported in university students, but high rates in young offenders on probation. Conformity rates apparently reflect the cultural expectations of participants and those of the experimenters.

- The 'stooges' in Asch-type experiments are usually seen as the majority. However, it may be more useful to see the naïve participant as embodying the 'conventional', self-evident, majority, whilst the 'stooges' reflect an unorthodox, unconventional, minority opinion. From this perspective, the minority influenced the majority 32 per cent of the time, and it is those participants who remained independent who are actually the conformists. This perspective is relevant to understanding how new ideas come to be accepted.

- A consistent minority can change the majority's view by drawing attention to itself as an entity, conveying the existence of an alternative, coherent point of view, and demonstrating certainty and a commitment to a particular point of view which represents the only solution to a current conflict.

- Minorities are also more effective if they display **investment**, **autonomy**, and a balance between **rigidity** and **flexibility**. They also have more influence if they are perceived as similar to the majority in terms of age, gender and social category.

- Both **informational social influence** (ISI) and **normative social influence** (NSI) operate in Asch-type experiments and other settings. Related to ISI is **internalisation** or **true conformity**, in which we say what we believe and believe what we say. Related to NSI is **compliance**, in which we say what we do not believe and do not believe what we say.

- The distinction between ISI and NSI has been called the **dual process dependency model of social influence**. However, this emphasises the **interpersonal** aspect of conformity experiments and underestimates the role of **group belongingness**. We may only experience uncertainty when we disagree with those with whom we expect to agree, especially those regarded as belonging to the same category/group and sharing certain characteristics and reactions (**referent informational influence**).

- Dissent may represent an attempt to remain independent as a matter of principle (**anticonformity**). Alternatively, it can be constructive and creative. Conformity may be a **rational judgement** by someone who does not have sufficient information on which to make a decision and so relies on others with greater expertise. However, failure to speak one's mind can be (mis)interpreted as support for something.

2 Introduction and overview

When people in authority tell us to do something, we tend to comply with their orders. For example, Cohen & Davis (1981, cited in Carlson, 1987) describe a case in which a physician prescribed ear drops for a patient with an ear infection and left instructions that the nurse should 'place drops in R ear'. However, the physician evidently did not leave a suitably big gap between the 'R' (for right) and the word 'ear'. Neither the nurse nor the patient questioned a treatment for earache in which the medication was delivered rectally.

The more serious *social* problems that obedience can cause have been described by Milgram (1974):

> 'From 1933 to 1945 millions of innocent persons were systematically slaughtered on command. Gas chambers were built, death camps were guarded, daily quotas of corpses were produced with the same efficiency as the manufacture of appliances. These inhuman policies may have originated in the mind of a single person, but they could only be carried out on a massive scale if a very large number of persons obeyed orders'.

This chapter looks at research into obedience, much of it conducted by Milgram, and considers what such research can tell us about why we are sometimes blindly obedient to others and how we might behave more independently.

Distinguishing between conformity and obedience

According to Milgram (1992), conformity and obedience are similar in that both involve the abdication of individual judgement in the face of some external pressure. However, there are at least three important differences between them. First, in conformity there is no *explicit* requirement to act in a certain way, whereas in obedience we are *ordered* or *instructed* to do something. Second, those who influence us when we conform are our *peers* (or *equals*), and people's behaviours become more alike because they are affected by *example*. In obedience, there is a difference in status from the outset and, rather than mutual influence, obedience is affected by *direction*, with somebody in *higher authority* influencing behaviour.

Third, conformity has to do with the psychological 'need' for acceptance by others and involves going along with one's peers in a group situation (see Chapter 1, page 13). Obedience, by contrast, has to do with the social power and status of an authority figure in a hierarchical situation. Although we typically deny that we are conformist (because it detracts from a sense of individuality), we usually deny *responsibility* for our behaviour in the case of obedience. As a result, behaviours occur because 'I was only following orders' (an explanation given by Adolf Eichmann, Director of the Nazi deportation of Jews to concentration camps) or because 'if the Commander in Chief tells this lieutenant colonel to go and stand in the corner and sit on his head, I will do so' (a response given by Oliver North in the Iran–Contra hearings of 1987).

Experimental studies: Milgram's research

The original purpose of Milgram's (1963, 1964, 1974) research was to test 'the "Germans are different" hypothesis'. This has been used by historians to explain the systematic destruction of millions of Jews, Poles and others by the Nazis during the 1930s and 1940s (see above). The hypothesis maintains that Hitler could not have put his evil plans into operation without the co-operation of thousands of others, and that the Germans have a basic character defect (namely, a readiness to obey authority without question, regardless of the acts demanded by the authority figure), which provided Hitler with the co-operation he needed. After piloting his research in America, Milgram planned to continue it in Germany to test for the existence of this hypothesised character defect. As will be seen, though, his results indicated that this was not necessary.

Milgram's participants

Originally, Milgram advertised for volunteers to take part in a study of learning to be conducted at Yale University. The experiment would last about an hour and participants would be paid $4.50 for their involvement. The first participants to be studied were 20–50-year-old men from all walks of life.

Public Announcement

WE WILL PAY YOU $4.00 FOR ONE HOUR OF YOUR TIME

Persons Needed for a Study of Memory

*We will pay five hundred New Haven men to help us complete a scientific study of memory and learning. The study is being done at Yale University.
*Each person who participates will be paid $4.00 (plus 50c carfare) for approximately 1 hour's time. We need you for only one hour: there are no further obligations. You may choose the time you would like to come (evenings, weekdays, or weekends).

*No special training, education, or experience is needed. We want:

Factory workers	Businessmen	Construction workers
City employees	Clerks	Salespeople
Laborers	Professional people	White-collar workers
Barbers	Telephone workers	Others

All persons must be between the ages of 20 and 50. High school and college students cannot be used.
*If you meet these qualifications, fill out the coupon below and mail it now to Professor Stanley Milgram, Department of Psychology, Yale University, New Haven. You will be notified later of the specific time and place of the study. We reserve the right to decline any application.
*You will be paid $4.00 (plus 50c carfare) as soon as you arrive at the laboratory.

- -

TO:
PROF. STANLEY MILGRAM, DEPARTMENT OF PSYCHOLOGY, YALE UNIVERSITY, NEW HAVEN, CONN. I want to take part in this study of memory and learning. I am between the ages of 20 and 50. I will be paid $4.00 (plus 50c carfare) if I participate.

NAME (Please Print). . . . .

ADDRESS . . . .

TELEPHONE NO. . . . . Best time to call you . . . .

AGE . . . . OCCUPATION . . . . SEX . . . . . .
CAN YOU COME:

WEEKDAYS . . . . EVENINGS . . . . . . WEEKENDS . . . .

Figure 2.1   *The advertisement used by Milgram to recruit participants for his study (From Milgram, 1974)*

The basic procedure

When participants arrived at Yale University's psychology department, they were met by a young, crew-cut man in a grey laboratory coat who introduced himself as Jack Williams, the experimenter. Also present was a Mr Wallace, a mild and harmless looking accountant in his late fifties. In fact, neither the experimenter nor Mr Wallace was genuine, and everything else that followed in the procedure (apart from the naïve participants' behaviour) was carefully pre-planned, staged and scripted. The participant and Mr Wallace were told that the experiment was concerned with the effects of punishment on learning, and that one of them would be the 'teacher' and the other the 'learner'. Their roles were determined by each drawing a piece of paper from a hat. In fact, both pieces of paper had 'teacher' written on them. Mr Wallace drew out the first and called out 'learner'. As a result, the real participant was always the 'teacher'. All three then went to an adjoining room, where the learner was strapped into a chair with his arms attached to electrodes that would supposedly deliver an electric shock from a generator in the adjacent room (see Figure 2.2).

The teacher and experimenter then went into the adjacent room. The teacher was shown the generator, which had a number of switches on it, each clearly marked with voltage levels and verbal descriptions. The shocks began at 15 volts and went up in 15-volt increments to 450 volts. The teacher was then given a 45-volt shock to convince him that the generator was real. However, and unknown to the teacher, this would be the only *actual* electric shock delivered during the whole experiment.

The task involved the teacher reading out a list of word pairs (such as 'blue–girl' and 'fat–neck'). After this, the first word of a pair was read out followed by a number of other words, one of which was the word it had been paired with. The learner had to choose the correct word by pressing one of four switches which turned on a light on a panel in the teacher's room. Each time the learner made a mistake, the teacher had to deliver a shock, with

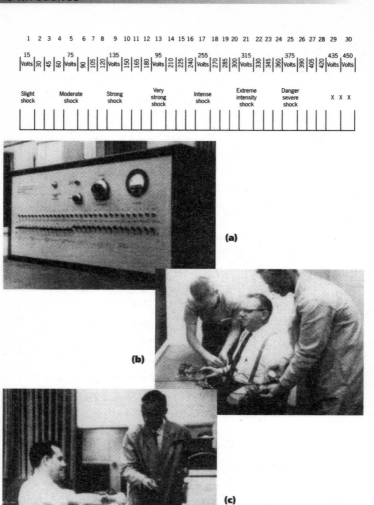

Figure 2.2 *(a) The 'electric shock generator' used by Milgram (left) and a schematic representation of its front panel showing the voltages and verbal labels (top). In (b), the 'learner' is strapped into his chair, and in (c), the 'teacher' receives a shock of 45 volts (From Milgram, 1974)*

each successive mistake being punished by a shock 15 volts higher than the previous one.

In Milgram's first experiment (the *remote victim* variation), the learner was scripted to pound loudly on the wall at 300 volts and, after 315 volts, to stop pounding on the wall *and* give no further answers. In the second experiment (the *voice feedback* variation), the teacher heard a tape-recorded series of verbal responses that were Mr Wallace's 'spontaneous reactions' to the increasing shock levels.

Box 2.1 *Mr Wallace's 'spontaneous reactions' to increasing shock levels administered by the teacher*

75, 90 and 105 volts: Makes a little grunt.

120 volts: Tells the experimenter that the shocks are becoming painful.

150 volts: Cries out 'Experimenter, get me out of here! I won't be in the experiment any more! I refuse to go on!'

180 volts: Shouts out 'I can't stand the pain!'

270 volts: Lets out an agonised scream and continues to insist on being released.

300 volts: Desperately shouts out that he will no longer provide answers.

315 volts: Lets out a violent scream and reaffirms vehemently that he will no longer provide answers.

330 volts: There is an ominous silence.

The scripted behaviours were, of course, dependent upon any participant actually continuing with the experiment up to that shock level. When Milgram asked his students what they thought would happen in the experiment, a few said that some people would continue all the way to 450 volts, but that most would stop early or in the middle of the shock range. Psychiatrists asked to predict the teachers' behaviour suggested that less than one per cent would administer the highest voltage, and that most would stop around 120 volts (Milgram, 1974).

The teacher had been instructed to treat a non-response from Mr Wallace (which, as Box 2.1 shows, occurred at 330 volts) as an incorrect response, so that shocks could continue to be given. Milgram's participants showed reluctance to administer the shocks and, whenever this happened, the experimenter gave a series of scripted 'verbal prods'. These were 'please continue' (or 'please go on'), 'the experiment requires that you continue', 'it is absolutely essential that you continue' and, finally, 'you have no other choice, you *must* go on'. The experimenter was also scripted to say 'although the shocks may be painful, there is no permanent tissue damage', in order to reassure the teacher that no permanent harm was being done to the learner. The experiment was terminated either when the participant refused to continue or when the maximum 450-volt shock had been administered four times.

Figure 2.3 *A participant refuses to continue any further with the experiment (From Milgram, 1974)*

Milgram's results

The participants displayed great anguish, verbally attacked the experimenter, twitched nervously, or broke out into nervous laughter. Many were observed to:

> 'sweat, stutter, tremble, groan, bite their lips and dig their nails into their flesh. Full-blown, uncontrollable seizures were observed for three [participants]' (Milgram, 1974).

Indeed, one experiment had to be stopped because the participant had a violent seizure. It is quite astonishing, then, that in the remote victim variation every teacher administered at least 300 volts and 65 per cent administered 450 volts. In the voice feedback variation, 62.5 per cent continued all the way up to 450 volts.

To determine why the obedience level was so high in these two studies, Milgram conducted a number of variations using the voice feedback condition as his baseline measure of obedience. In all, a further 16 variations were conducted.

Box 2.2 *Some variations on Milgram's basic procedure*

Institutional context (variation 10): In post-experimental interviews, many participants said they continued administering shocks because the experiment was being conducted at Yale University, a highly prestigious institution. However, when Milgram transferred the experiment to a rundown office in downtown Bridgeport, the 450 volt obedience rate was 47.5 per cent. This suggests that whilst the institutional context played a role, it was not a crucial factor.

Proximity and touch proximity (variations 3 and 4): In the original variation, the teacher and learner were in adjacent rooms and could not see one another. However, when they were in the same room (about 1.5 feet/46 cm apart), the 450 volt obedience rate dropped to 40 per cent (variation 3). When the teacher was required to force the learner's hand down onto a shock plate (variation 4), the 450 volt obedience rate dropped to 30 per cent. Whilst seeing the effects of the shock on the participant reduces obedience, the figures observed are still very high.

Remote authority (variation 7): When the experimenter left the room (having given the essential instructions), and gave subsequent instructions by telephone, 450 volt obedience dropped to 20.5 per cent. Indeed, participants often pretended to administer a shock or administered a shock lower than they were supposed to. This suggests they were trying to compromise between their conscience and the experimenter's instructions. In his absence, it was easier to follow their conscience.

Two peers rebel (variation 17): In this variation, the teacher was paired with two other (actor) teachers. The teachers read out the list of word-pairs and informed the learner if the response was correct. The real participant administered the shocks. At 150 volts, the first teacher refused to continue and moved to another part of the room. At 210 volts, the second teacher did likewise. The experimenter ordered the real teacher to continue. Only ten per cent of participants continued to 450 volts. Most stopped obeying when the first or second teacher refused to continue. According to Milgram (1965):

> 'the effects of peer rebellion are most impressive in undercutting the experimenter's authority'.

A peer administers the shocks (variation 18): When the teacher was paired with another teacher (an actor) and had only to read out the word-pairs rather than administer the shock, obedience rose to 92.5 per cent. This shows that it is easier for participants to shift responsibility from themselves to the other teacher.

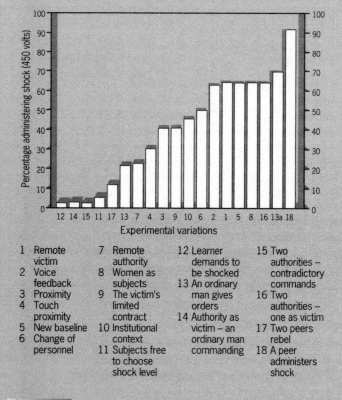

1 Remote victim
2 Voice feedback
3 Proximity
4 Touch proximity
5 New baseline
6 Change of personnel
7 Remote authority
8 Women as subjects
9 The victim's limited contract
10 Institutional context
11 Subjects free to choose shock level
12 Learner demands to be shocked
13 An ordinary man gives orders
14 Authority as victim – an ordinary man commanding
15 Two authorities – contradictory commands
16 Two authorities – one as victim
17 Two peers rebel
18 A peer administers shock

Figure 2.4   *The percentage of participants administering 450-volt shocks across the 18 variations of Milgram's original experiment. Note that one experiment has two variations (13 and 13a) (From Zimbardo & Weber, 1994)*

Explaining Milgram's results

According to Milgram (1974):

> 'the most fundamental lesson of our study is that ordinary people, simply doing their jobs, and without any particular hostility on their part, can become agents in a terrible destructive process'.

A number of explanations as to why people obey have been proposed.

The set-up's credibility

Participants might not have believed the experimental set-up they found themselves in, and knew the learner was not really being given electric shocks. Sheridan & King's (1972) study appears to exclude this possibility. They had students train a puppy to learn a discrimination task by punishing it with increasingly severe and *real* electric shocks each time it made an error. Although the puppy received only a small shock, it could be seen and its squeals heard by the participants.

After a time, an odourless anaesthetic was released into the puppy's cage, causing it to fall asleep. Although participants complained about the procedure (and some even cried), they were reminded that failure to respond was a punishable error and that shocks should continue to be given. Seventy-five per cent of participants delivered the maximum shock possible. Clearly, then, it is unlikely that Milgram's procedure leads participants to believe that the learner is not really being harmed, and so the experiment has *experimental realism* (Orne & Holland, 1968).

Demand characteristics

Another possibility is that cues in the experimental setting influenced the participants' perceptions of what was required of them. Obedience might, then, simply have been a response to the demands of the unusual experimental setting (Zimbardo & Weber, 1994). Naturalistic studies of obedience, however, dispute this and indicate that Milgram's research also has *mundane realism* (Orne & Holland, 1968), in that its results extend beyond the laboratory setting. For example, Hofling *et al.* (1966) showed that when nurses were instructed by telephone to administer twice the maximum dosage of a drug (actually a harmless tablet) to a patient, 21 out of 22 did so. Even when there are good reasons to defy authority, then, it is hard to resist it (Zimbardo & Weber, 1994).

Personal responsibility

Many participants raised the issue of responsibility should harm befall the learner. Although the experimenter did not always discuss this, when he did say 'I'm responsible for what goes on here', participants showed visible relief. Indeed, when participants are told that *they* are responsible for what happens, obedience is sharply reduced (Hamilton, 1978). Milgram saw this *diffusion of responsibility* as being crucial to understanding the Nazi atrocities of people like Eichmann, and his defence that he was 'just carrying out orders'. It can also explain the behaviour of William Calley, an American soldier who was court-martialed for the 1968 massacre by troops under his command of several hundred Vietnam civilians at My Lai (Opton, 1973).

The perception of legitimate authority

As mentioned earlier (see page 26), many participants showed signs of distress and conflict in Milgram's experiments, and so the diffusion of responsibility explanation cannot tell the whole story. Perhaps, then, the experimenter was seen as a legitimate authority by participants, at least up until the point when he said 'you have no other choice, you *must* go on'. The most common mental adjustment in the obedient participant is to see him/herself as an agent of external authority (the *agentic state*). This state (the opposite of an *autonomous state*) is what allows us to function in an organised and hierarchical social system. For a group to function as a whole, individuals must give up responsibility and defer to others of higher status in the social hierarchy. Legitimate authority thus replaces a person's own self-regulation (Turner, 1991).

Authority figures often possess highly visible symbols of their power or status that make it difficult to refuse their commands. In Milgram's experiments, the experimenter always wore a grey laboratory coat to indicate his position as an authority figure. The impact of such 'visible symbols' has been demonstrated by Bickman (1974), who showed that when people are told by a person in a guard's uniform to pick up a paper bag or give a coin to a stranger, obedience is higher (80 per cent) than when the instruction is given by somebody in civilian clothes (40 per cent). For Milgram:

'a substantial proportion of people do what they are told to do, irrespective of the content of the act and without limitations of conscience, so long as they perceive that the command comes from a legitimate authority'.

Box 2.3 *Obedience to authority in a simulated prison*

Zimbardo *et al.* (1973) recruited participants through newspaper advertisements asking for student volunteers for a two-week study of prison life. After potential participants had been given clinical interviews, 25 of over 100 who volunteered were selected. They were all judged to be emotionally stable, physically healthy, 'normal to average' on the basis of personality tests, and also law abiding.

Participants were told that they would be randomly assigned to the role of either 'prisoner' or 'guard' (although all had stated a preference for being a prisoner). At the beginning of the study, then, there were no differences between those selected to be prisoners and guards. They were a relatively homogeneous group of white, middle class college students from all over America and Canada.

Zimbardo *et al.* converted the basement of the Stanford University psychology department into a 'mock prison'. It was made as much like a real prison as possible in an attempt to simulate functionally some of the significant features of the psychological state of imprisonment. The experiment began one Sunday morning, when those allocated to the 'prisoner' role were unexpectedly arrested by the local police. They were charged with a felony, read their rights, searched, handcuffed, and taken to the police station to be 'booked'. After being fingerprinted, and having forms prepared for their central information file, each prisoner was taken blindfold to the 'prison'.

Upon arrival, the prisoners were stripped naked, skin-searched, deloused, and issued a uniform and bedding. They wore a loose-fitting smock with an identification number on the front and back, plus a chain bolted around one ankle. They also wore nylon stockings to cover their hair (in a real prison, their hair would have been shaved off). The prisoners were referred to by their numbers and housed in 639-foot (191.7-metre) cells, three to a cell. The guards wore military-style khaki uniforms, silver reflector sunglasses (making eye contact with them impossible) and carried clubs, whistles, handcuffs and keys to the cells and main gate. The guards were on duty 24 hours a day, in eight-hour shifts, and had complete control over the prisoners. The prisoners were imprisoned around the clock, and allowed out of their cells only for meals, exercise, toilet privileges, head counts and work.

After an initial 'rebellion' had been crushed, the prisoners began to react passively as the guards stepped up their aggression each day (by, for example, having a roll call in the middle of the night simply to disrupt the prisoners' sleep). This made the prisoners feel helpless, and no longer in control of their lives.

The guards began to enjoy their power. As one said, 'Acting authoritatively can be great fun. Power can be a great pleasure'. After less than 36 hours, one prisoner had to be released because of uncontrolled crying, fits of rage, disorganised thinking and severe depression. Three others developed the same symptoms and had to be released on successive days. Another prisoner developed a rash over his whole body, which was triggered when his attempt to get 'parole' was rejected. Prisoners became demoralised and apathetic, and even began to refer to themselves and others by their prison numbers.

The whole experiment, planned to run for two weeks, was stopped after *six days* because of the pathological reactions of the prisoners who had originally been selected for their emotional stability. An outside observer, who had a long history of being incarcerated, reported that the mock prison and both the guards' and prisoners' behaviours were strikingly similar to real life. One conclusion which can be drawn from this study is that the distinction between *role-playing* and *role enactment* is a very fine one.

The 'foot in the door' and not knowing how to disobey

According to Gilbert (1981), participants in Milgram's experiments may have been 'sucked in' by the series of graduated demands, which began with seemingly innocuous orders that gradually escalated. It is possible that having begun the experiment, participants found it difficult to extricate themselves from it. They may even not have known *how* to disobey, since nothing they said had any effect on the experimenter (at least until they refused the final verbal 'prod' in which they were told they had no choice but to continue).

Socialisation

Despite our expressed ideal of independence, obedience is something we are socialised into from a very early age by significant others (including our parents and teachers). Obedience may be an *ingrained habit* (Brown, 1986) that is difficult to resist.

An evaluation of Milgram's research

Not surprisingly, Milgram's results caused much interest when they were published. Critics have largely focused on three main areas, namely *methodological issues*, *issues of generalisation*, and *ethical issues*.

Methodological issues

One criticism made of Milgram's research was that his sample was *unrepresentative*. However, Milgram studied a total of 636 participants in his experiments, representing a cross-section of New Haven's population, thought to be a fairly typical small

American town. However, Milgram did concede that those participants who continued administering shocks up to 450 volts were more likely to see the learner as being responsible for what happened to him rather than themselves. These participants seemed to have a stronger authoritarian character, which includes a respect for authority as such, and a less advanced level of moral development, although this was a matter of degree only. Indeed, people who volunteer for experiments (as, of course, Milgram's participants did) tend to be considerably *less* authoritarian than those who do not (Rosenthal & Rosnow, 1966).

Milgram was also criticised for using mainly male participants. However, of the 40 females who did serve as participants (in variation 8), 65 per cent continued administering shocks up to 450 volts, a figure comparable to the obedience shown by their male counterparts. A further methodological criticism concerns the cross-cultural replicability of Milgram's findings. Studies conducted in many countries have produced various obedience rates ranging from 16 per cent (Kilham & Mann, 1974, using female Australian students) to 92 per cent (Meeus & Raaijmakers, 1986, using members of the general Dutch population).

Issues of generalisation

Several researchers have argued that whilst Milgram's experiments had high *internal validity*, his results would not prevail in other circumstances. The charge here is that Milgram's findings lack *external* or *ecological validity* (or *mundane realism*: see page 29). According to Milgram, though, the essential process in complying with the demands of an authority figure is the same whether the setting is the artificial one of the psychological laboratory or a naturally occurring one outside it, a point accepted by many researchers (e.g. Colman, 1987).

There are, of course, differences between laboratory studies of obedience and the obedience observed in Nazi Germany. However, as Milgram (1974) has remarked in this context:

'differences in scale, numbers and political context may turn out to be relatively unimportant as long as certain essential features are retained. The essence of obedience consists in the fact that a person comes to view himself as the instrument for carrying out another person's wishes, and he, therefore, no longer regards himself as responsible for his actions. Once this critical shift of viewpoint has occurred in the person, all the essential features of obedience follow'.

Hofling *et al.*'s (1966) study, which showed that 95 per cent of nurses studied complied with an instruction that involved them infringing both hospital regulations and medical ethics (see page 30), indicates that obedience is not a phenomenon that is confined to the setting of Milgram's laboratory.

Unfortunately, the available data are not particularly helpful in allowing us to comment on cross-cultural similarities or differences in obedience. One reason is that the replications undertaken have only been *partial*, and have not completely duplicated Milgram's procedures. For example, in Kilham & Mann's (1974) study, the female participants were required to administer the electric shocks to another *female*. In Milgram's experiments, however, the learner was always a *male* (Smith & Bond, 1993). Humphreys (1994) identifies other differences in cross-cultural studies of obedience. These include the use of a maximum shock value of 330 volts rather than 450 volts (Ancona & Pareyson, 1968), and the use of a long-haired student as the learner rather than a 'Mr Wallace'-type character (Kilham & Mann, 1974).

Ethical issues

One of Milgram's strongest critics was Baumrind (1964), who argued that the rights and feelings of Milgram's participants had been abused and that inadequate measures were taken to protect participants from stress and emotional conflict. Whilst accepting that participants did experience stress and conflict in his experiment, Milgram countered that Baumrind's criticism presupposes that the experiment's outcome was *expected*, which, of course, it was not (at least not by those students and psychiatrists asked to anticipate what might happen: see page 25).

Inducing stress was not an intended and deliberate effect of the experimental procedure. As Milgram (1974) noted:

'understanding grows because we examine situations in which the end is unknown. An investigator unwilling to accept this degree of risk must give up the idea of scientific enquiry'.

An experimenter cannot, then, know what the results are going to be before the experiment begins.

Box 2.4 *Deception*

A further ethical issue concerns *deception*. According to Vitelli (1988), more than one third of social psychological studies (and virtually all of those that investigate conformity and obedience) deceive participants over the research's purpose, the accuracy of the information they are given, and/or the true identity of a person they believe to be another genuine participant (or experimenter).

In his defence, Milgram pointed out that, after learning about the deception when they were extensively debriefed, 84 per cent of participants said they were glad or very glad to have participated, whereas fewer than two per cent said they were sorry or very sorry to have participated. Moreover, 80 per cent said they felt *more* experiments of this kind should be conducted, and 74 per cent felt that they had learned something of personal importance after being a participant.

Other researchers have defended Milgram's use of deception on the grounds that if he had not used it, he would have found results which simply do not reflect how people behave when they are led to believe they are in real situations (Aronson, 1988). In some circumstances, then, deception may be the best (and perhaps the only) way to get useful information about how people behave in complex and important situations.

What do Milgram's studies tell us about ourselves?

Perhaps one of the reasons Milgram's research was criticised is that it paints an unacceptable picture of humans. Thus, it is far easier for us to accept that a war criminal like Adolf Eichmann was an inhuman impostor than that 'ordinary people' can be destructively obedient. Yet atrocities, such as those committed in Rwanda and the former Yugoslavia, continue to occur. Perhaps, like the 51 per cent of those people questioned following the trial and conviction of William Calley (see page 30) who said they would behave in the same way if commanded, 'we do as we are told'. Such actions may be seen as:

'normal, even desirable because [people like Calley] performed them in obedience to legitimate authority' (Kelman & Lawrence, 1972).

Box 2.5 *Genocide*

Hirsch (1995) has noted that many of the greatest crimes against humanity are committed in the name of obedience. *Genocide*, a term coined in 1944, tends to occur under conditions created by three social processes. The first of these, *authorisation*, relates to the 'agentic state' (see page 30), that is, obeying orders because of where they come from. The second, *routinisation*, refers to massacre becoming a matter of routine, or a mechanical and highly programmed operation. The third is *dehumanisation*, in which the victims are reduced to something less than human which allows us to suspend our usual moral prohibition on killing (see Humphreys, 1994).

The ingredients of genocide were personified by Eichmann who, at his trial after the Second World War, denied ever killing anybody, but took great pride in the way he transported millions to their death 'with great zeal and meticulous care' (Arendt, 1965). The comments of an East German judge in 1992, when sentencing a former East German border guard for having shot a man trying (three years earlier) to escape to the West, echo the spirit of the Nuremberg Accords which followed the Nazi war crimes trials:

'Not everything that is legal is right ... At the end of the twentieth century, no one has the right to turn off his conscience when it comes to killing people on the orders of authorities' (cited in Berkowitz, 1993).

As noted, it is difficult to disobey authority. However, we are most likely to rebel when we feel that social pressure is so strong that our *freedom* is in danger of being lost. In one demonstration of this, Gamson *et al.* (1982) invited the citizens of a midwestern town to a hotel conference centre in order to discuss community standards. The researchers explained that a local petrol station manager had publicly opposed high petrol prices and that the petrol company was taking legal action against him. The participants were led to believe that an oil company was videotaping the group discussion, and were asked to speak out against the petrol station manager and to allow their taped discussions to be used in court. The researchers then left the participants. The participants reacted strongly to this threat to their freedom (even citing Milgram's research to justify their behaviour!). They strongly defended the station manager and refused to give in to the oil company's demands. Some participants even made plans to report the company, whilst others decided to tell their story to the newspapers.

Milgram himself felt that by *educating* people about the dangers of blind obedience, encouraging them to *question authority*, and exposing them to the actions of *disobedient models*, obedience would be reduced. Other researchers have emphasised the importance of *reactance*. According to Brehm (1966), we need to believe that we have freedom of choice. When we believe that this is not the case and when we believe we are *entitled* to freedom, we experience reactance, an unpleasant emotional state. To reduce this state, and restore the sense of freedom, disobedience occurs.

Conclusions

As is apparent in this chapter, there are circumstances in which we can become what Milgram calls 'agents in a terrible destructive process'. However, we are not *always* blindly obedient. Social psychology's task is to continue uncovering those situations in which such destructive obedience occurs and to look at how it can be prevented.

Summary

- Conformity and obedience are similar in some important respects but different in others. In obedience, we are ordered or instructed to do something by somebody higher in authority. Typically, we **deny responsibility** for our behaviours when we are obedient.

- Important research into obedience was conducted by Milgram, who originally intended to test the 'Germans are different' hypothesis. In Milgram's basic procedure, participants are led to believe that they will be delivering increasingly severe electric shocks to another person in a learning experiment. In fact, no shocks are actually given, and neither the learner nor the experimenter in charge is genuine.

- In Milgram's **remote victim variation**, 65 per cent of participants administered the maximum 450-volt shock. In the **voice feedback condition**, the figure was 62.5 per cent. These results were unexpected. When Milgram asked psychiatrists and students to predict participants' behaviour, few believed anyone would administer the maximum shock.

- Participants were given pre-determined 'verbal prods' by the experimenter when they showed a reluctance to continue. Despite being reassured that no permanent harm was being done to the learner, participants showed great anguish and experienced considerable stress. One experiment had to be stopped due to a participant's violent seizure.

- Milgram conducted 16 further variations of the two original studies to determine the factors influencing obedience. **Proximity**, **touch proximity**, **remote authority**, **peer rebellion** and changing the **institutional context** all reduced obedience to various degrees. Having a **peer administer shocks**, however, increased obedience.

- It is unlikely that Milgram's procedure led participants to believe that the learner was not really being harmed, and so the experiment has **experimental realism**. It is unlikely that demand characteristics account for the findings, since obedience has been observed in naturalistic settings. So, Milgram's research has **mundane realism**.

- When participants are told **they** are responsible for what happens to the learner, obedience is sharply reduced. Milgram saw **diffusion of responsibility** as crucial to understanding destructive obedience. The perception of the experimenter as a **legitimate authority**, which induces an **agentic state**, also contributes to obedient behaviour.

- People's tendency to obey those perceived as legitimate authorities was dramatically shown in Zimbardo *et al.*'s 'prison simulation' experiment. Since obedience is an **ingrained habit** acquired through early **socialisation**, Milgram's participants might not have known how to disobey.

- Milgram's research has been criticised on **methodological grounds**, although none of the criticisms destroys its credibility. Whilst it has high **internal validity**, critics contend that the research lacks **external/ecological validity**. Although there are obvious differences between obedience observed in laboratory experiments and natural settings, Milgram believes that the **essential features** are the same for both.

- The most serious objections to Milgram's research have been **ethical**. Charges of failing to protect participants from harm can be dismissed, because distress could not have been anticipated.

- Milgram defended his use of **deception** by pointing out that participants were extensively debriefed. Eighty-four per cent said they were glad/very glad to have participated, and only two per cent said they were sorry/very sorry. Deception may be unavoidable if we are to obtain information about how people behave in complex and important situations.

- Milgram's studies indicate that ordinary people can be destructively obedient. Many of the greatest crimes have been committed in the name of obedience. **Genocide** tends to occur under conditions created by **authorisation, routinisation** and **dehumanisation**.

- Whilst it is difficult to disobey authority, we are most likely to rebel when we feel our **freedom** is being threatened. Disobedience can occur when we try to reduce **reactance** and restore the sense of freedom.

- Milgram believed that obedience can be reduced by **educating** people about the dangers of blind obedience, encouraging them to **question authority**, and exposing them to **disobedient models**.

SOCIAL POWER: LEADERS AND LEADERSHIP

3

Introduction and overview

Hollander (1985) defines a *leader* as the person who exercises the most influence in a group, and *leadership* as the exercise of influence or power over others. The earliest research in this area attempted to identify the individual qualities that result in some people rising to positions of power and authority. Thus, the concern was with whether leaders are born or made and what it is about leaders, compared with followers, that makes them leaders. This focus on 'the leader' is often referred to as the *trait approach*.

Later research concentrated on identifying the conditions which influence the effectiveness of those who are appointed to a formal leadership role, and was typically carried out in large organisations (such as businesses). This is often referred to as the *situational approach*, since it acknowledges that leadership is a complex social process in which the leader depends on the group and *vice versa*. This chapter reviews theory and research relating to the emergence of leaders, and the factors affecting their leadership once they have assumed a position of power and authority.

Leaders: traits, situations and transactions

Traits and leader emergence

For many years, theorising on the emergence of leaders was dominated by the 'great person' or *trait theory*. According to this, leaders are extraordinary people who naturally rise to positions of power and authority because they possess certain personality traits which suit them for 'life at the top'. For Huczynski & Buchanan (1991):

'the fate of societies ... is in the hands of key, powerful, idiosyncratic individuals who by the force of their personalities reach positions of influence from which they can direct and dominate the lives of others. Such men are simply born great and emerge to take power in any situation regardless of the social or historical context'.

In a review of the research, Stogdill (1974) looked at leadership in various contexts, including the military, nursery schools, and political parties. Stogdill concluded that leaders tend to be slightly more intelligent, sociable, achievement oriented, experienced, older and taller than their followers. Other studies have shown that people who emerge as leaders tend to score higher on measures of self-confidence and dominance (Costantini & Craik, 1980) and combine orientations towards success and affiliating with other people (Sorrentino & Field, 1986).

Evidence of particular traits in leaders has, however, been mixed and, in general, leaders have *not* been shown to be consistently different from non-leaders in terms of their personality traits (Turner, 1991). Whilst claims continue to be made about the characteristics that separate leaders from non-leaders (e.g. Kirkpatrick & Locke, 1991), it is generally agreed that the trait approach to leadership is limited, and that the kinds of traits a leader needs will vary from group to group and problem to problem.

Situations and leader emergence

The view that different kinds of traits are needed in different situations was examined by Bales (1950), who stressed the *functional demands* of the situation. According to this perspective, the person most likely to emerge as a leader is the one who is best equipped to help the group fulfil its objectives in a particular context. Thus, the leader will be the one whose *skills* and *competence* are most useful to the group in a given situation. At another time, and in another situation, someone else may be more suited for the leader's role. A good example of this comes from Sherif *et al.*'s (1961) Robber's Cave field experiment (see Gross & McIlveen, 1998) in which, when competition between two groups of boys was increased, one of the groups replaced its leader with a physically much stronger boy.

Whilst there is evidence consistent with the view that the situation determines who will emerge as a leader, this approach assumes that under the appropriate conditions *anyone* can become a leader. However, the evidence does not support this, and whilst personality factors may not be as crucial as the trait approach proposes, it seems that some people adopt the role of a leader more readily than others (Nydegger, 1975). Also, people seem to be fairly well aware of their relative abilities to assume positions of power and authority.

Transactions and leader emergence

In recent years, *transactional theory* (Shaw, 1981) has been applied to both the trait and situational approaches to leader emergence. According to this, both the characteristics of people *and* the demands of the situation determine who will become a leader. This approach to leaders is looked at more closely in the section on *leader effectiveness*.

Leadership style and behaviour

Autocratic, democratic and laissez-faire styles

An early study of leadership style was conducted by Lewin *et al.* (1939). They wanted to investigate the effects of three different kinds of adult behaviour on a group of ten-year-old boys attending after-school clubs. The clubs, which were concerned with model making, were led by adults who acted *autocratically*, *democratically* or in a *laissez-faire* manner.

Box 3.1 *The behaviour of the adults in Lewin* et al.*'s study*

Autocratic leaders told the boys what sort of models they would make and with whom they would work. They sometimes praised or

---

blamed the boys for their work but did not explain their comments and, although friendly, were also aloof and impersonal.

Democratic leaders discussed various possible projects with the boys, and allowed them to choose whom they would work with and to make their own decisions. The leaders explained their comments and joined in with the group activities.

Laissez-faire leaders left the boys very much to their own devices, and only offered help when asked for it (which was not very often) and gave neither praise nor blame.

The boys with an *autocratic* leader became aggressive towards each other when things went wrong and were submissive in their approaches to the leader (and these approaches were often attention-seeking). If the leader left the room, the boys stopped working and became either disruptive or apathetic. However, the models they made were comparable, in terms of both quantity and quality, to those produced by the boys with the democratic leader.

Whilst the boys with the *democratic leader* actually produced slightly less work than those with the autocratic leader, they got on much better and seemed to like each other much more than did the boys with the autocratic leader. Any approaches made to the leader tended to be task-related, and when the leader left the room, the boys carried on working and showed greater independence. They also co-operated when things went wrong.

Like the boys with the autocratic leader, those with the *laissez-faire leader* were aggressive towards each other (although slightly less than the former). The boys also got very little work done, whether the leader was present or not, and were easily discouraged from finding solutions when things did not go exactly right for them.

The leader was changed every seven weeks and adopted one of the other kinds of leadership style. Thus, each group of boys was exposed to the same leadership style which was enacted by three different leaders. This was meant to ensure that the boys' behaviour could be attributed to leadership style rather than the leader's personality traits. Interestingly, when two of the most aggressive boys from the autocratic group were switched to the democratic group, they quickly became cooperative and involved in the tasks.

Lewin *et al.*'s findings suggest that it is leadership style (which is not necessarily a fixed characteristic) that is important, rather than the leader's personality (which is). However, people, their groups and leaders, can only really be understood in the context of the wider society of which they form a part (Brown, 1985). The democratic style is, implicitly, the most favourable and acceptable one of the three studied by Lewin *et al.*, because that style was the prevalent one in American society during the 1930s.

The results of many experimental and survey studies looking at the effects of these leadership styles in industrial settings were reviewed by Sayles (1966). No one style was consistently superior to any other in experimental studies of supervisors, but survey studies showed the democratic style to be associated with greater productivity and more acceptable than an autocratic style. However, Sayles argued that the tasks used in the experimental studies were so boring and limited that people did not really get involved in them. As a result, differences in leadership style were not really given the opportunity to show up. Sayles also pointed out that democratic supervisors probably differ from autocratic supervisors in ways other than leadership style (such as level of intelligence).

Initiating structure and showing consideration

One of the largest-ever leadership studies was conducted by Halpin & Winer (1952). They asked people in many different kinds of groups what they felt were the most important behaviours a leader should exhibit. Two major categories emerged. The first was called *initiating structure*, which means that a leader should define the goals of the group, plan how those goals should be achieved, indicate how each member of the group will be involved, and generally direct the action of the whole group. The second was called *showing consideration*. This involves communicating with individual members of the group, explaining why certain actions have been taken, and demonstrating positive regard for group members.

Initiating structure involves giving orders, telling people what to do, getting the task underway and, perhaps, 'ruffling a few feathers'. Showing consideration involves listening and explaining to group members, making people feel better and, perhaps, 'smoothing feathers'. These two behaviours can be difficult, though not impossible, for one person to show. This incompatibility, coupled with the finding that leaders have somewhat different traits in different situations, led researchers to try to identify leaders according to whether they primarily initiate structure or show consideration.

Task specialists and socioemotional specialists

Research into the leadership patterns that emerge in small, unstructured groups was undertaken by Bales & Slater (1955). They studied a group of college students who spent about five hours per day discussing and trying to come up with solutions for a number of labour-management conflicts. At the end of each day, the students were required to indicate which person in the group had come up with the best ideas, which had most effectively guided the group discussion, and how much they liked each group member.

Box 3.2 *The results of Bales and Slater's study*

Bales and Slater found that at the end of the first day, the person who was most liked was also the person rated as having the best ideas and making the greatest contribution to moving group discussion towards a successful task solution. However, after the first day, the tendency for the best-liked person also to be the one rated as having the best ideas diminished rapidly. What apparently happened on the following days was that two leaders emerged. One of these, the *task specialist*, made suggestions, provided information and expressed opinions. The other, the *socioemotional specialist*, helped other group members express themselves, cracked jokes, released tension, and expressed positive feelings for others.

Bales and Slater's task specialist style corresponds to the 'initiating structure' behaviour identified by Halpin and Winer. The socioemotional style corresponds to the 'showing consideration' behaviour. Bales and Slater believed that these styles were *inversely related* and that no one person could display both of them simultaneously. However, the results from the Ohio State Leadership studies (e.g. Stogdill, 1974) suggested that the two styles are *independent dimensions* and that the most effective leaders are those who score above average on both. Later studies have tended to confirm this. For example, Sorrentino & Field (1986) carried out detailed observations of 12 problem-solving groups over a five-week period. Those members who scored high on both of Bales and Slater's styles were subsequently elected leaders by the group members.

Another interesting finding concerns the relationship enjoyed by the two types of leader. Whilst there is rivalry between them, they get along well and co-operate extensively (Crider *et al.*, 1989). However, and as Crider *et al.* note, the general tendency to split leadership in unstructured groups has one qualification. According to Bales and Slater, the split happens only *after* the task specialist is identified and agreed upon. Once it has been decided who will lead the group in pursuit of its goal, the group can afford the luxury of a socioemotional leader.

Fiedler's contingency model of leader effectiveness

In his review of research concerning leadership effectiveness, Shaw (1981) claimed that both autocratic (or task specialist) leaders and democratic (or socioemotional specialist) leaders can be effective. In terms of group dynamics, followers are clearly happier in groups with socioemotional leaders. In terms of productivity, however, task specialist leaders are, on average, more successful.

However, Shaw made some important qualifications to this. For example, the productivity of groups with socioemotional leaders is highly variable, and both the most and the least productive groups can have socioemotional leaders. Because evidence suggests that both task specialist and socioemotional leaders are more effective, researchers have looked at the possibility that each style may be more advantageous in different situations.

The *contingency model of leader effectiveness*, first proposed by Fiedler (1964, 1981; Fiedler & Chemers, 1984), is mainly concerned with the fit or match between a leader's personal qualities (or leadership style) and the requirements of the situation in which the group must operate. Fiedler began by measuring the extent to which leaders distinguished between their most and least preferred co-workers (LPC). Fiedler then developed a scale to produce a LPC score.

Box 3.3 *Fiedler's LPC scale*

A leader is asked to think of all those people (or subordinates) who have ever worked under him or her, and to select the one that was the most difficult to work with. This person is then rated on 18 bipolar scales including 'pleasant' – 'unpleasant', 'trustworthy' – 'untrustworthy', and 'friendly' – 'unfriendly'. The sum of the values on the 18 scales gives a LPC score.

The LPC scale is arranged so that leaders with a high LPC score still see their least preferred co-workers in a relatively favourable light. Leaders with a low LPC score have a very negative attitude towards their least preferred co-workers. Those with high LPC scores tend to be more accepting, permissive, considerate and person oriented in their relationships with group members (*relationship-oriented leaders*). Those with low LPC scores tend to be directive, controlling and dominant in relationships with group members (*task-oriented leaders*).

Fiedler then investigated the fit between the two leadership styles identified in Box 3.3 and the situation in which the group must operate. His basic hypothesis was that a leader's effectiveness is *contingent* upon the fit between the leader's style and the degree of 'favourableness' of the situation (the extent to which the situation allows the leader to exert influence). The degree of favourableness of the situation is determined by three situational variables, each of which can have a high or low value. These are *quality of leader–member relationships, task structure,* and *position-power*. Fiedler sees the first of these as being most important, and the third as least.

Box 3.4 *The three situational variables that influence a situation's degree of favourableness*

Quality of leader–member relationships: This is the extent to which the leader has the loyalty and confidence of group members, and the group's general psychological atmosphere.

Task structure: This is the clarity and complexity of the task and the number of possible solutions. The more unstructured the task is, the more the leader must motivate and inspire members to find solutions.

Position-power: This is the power inherent in the leader's role, such as the rewards and punishments at his or her disposal, and the organisational support from superiors.

How combinations of these factors (according to whether they are high or low) covary to produce conditions which are favourable or unfavourable to the leader is shown in Figure 3.1. Fiedler hypothesised that task-oriented leaders will be most effective in situations which are either highly favourable (the values of the three situational variables are high) or highly unfavourable (the values are low). Relationship-oriented leaders will be more effective when the degree of favourableness is neither very high nor very low.

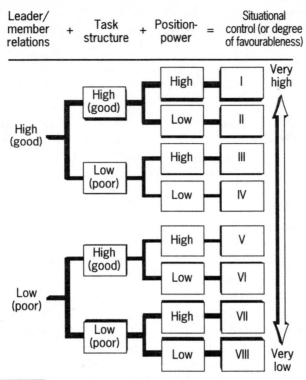

| Leader/member relations | + | Task structure | + | Position-power | = | Situational control (or degree of favourableness) |

Figure 3.1 *The covariation of factors producing varying degrees of favourability for a leader (From Gross, 1996)*

The rationale for these hypotheses is that when the situation is very favourable, task-oriented leaders do not have to waste any time worrying about the group members' morale, and an emphasis on interpersonal relations is not only unnecessary but may even irritate the group. In highly unfavourable situations, a task-oriented style is necessary since, without an emphasis on production, the group may fall apart. When conditions are moderately favourable or unfavourable, a relationship-oriented style may be able to smooth over differences of opinion in the group and improve co-operation enough to compensate for an ill-defined task and a lack of authority (Brown, 1988).

An evaluation of Fiedler's model

According to Fiedler (1967):

'except perhaps for the unusual case, it is simply not meaningful to speak of an effective or an ineffective leader; we can only speak of a leader who tends to be effective in one situation and ineffective in another'.

Fiedler has studied leadership in a wide range of groups including store managers, research chemists, basketball players, furnace workers, and bomber crews, and reported data consistent with his model's predictions. Other researchers, too, agree that there is considerable empirical support for the model (e.g. Greenberg & Baron, 1995), although this is stronger from laboratory than field studies.

Perhaps one reason the data have not always offered strong support for the model concerns some of the assumptions it makes. For example, Fiedler claims that leadership style is a relatively fixed characteristic of the leader (part of the leader's personality). As a result, leaders would be expected to find it difficult to modify their leadership styles. However, the test–retest reliability of LPC scores has been found to be low (Rice, 1978), suggesting that leadership style can change.

Another criticism concerns Fiedler's assumption that the most important of the three situational variables is the quality of the leader–follower relationship, and the least important the leader's legitimate power (see Box 3.6). It is not clear on what basis this assumption has been made, and the relative importance of the three situational variables could be a function of contextual factors (Hogg & Vaughan, 1995).

Hogg and Vaughan also argue that the contingency model ignores the group processes responsible for the rise and fall of leaders and the situational complexity of leadership. Despite these criticisms, though, there is little doubt that Fiedler's model has been useful in helping us begin to understand leadership effectiveness. As additional leadership qualities (such as intelligence and prior experience) are incorporated into the model, so a more complete picture will emerge (Smith, 1995).

Leadership as a process

Leadership involves leaders *and* followers in various role relationships, and there are several paths to becoming *validated* as a leader. The issue of validation concerns how a leader comes to occupy the role (how he or she achieves *legitimacy* as a leader). In a formal group structure, the leader is assigned by an external authority and is imposed on the group. Such a person is an *appointed leader*. In an informal group, however, the leader achieves authority from the group members (who may withdraw their support just as they gave it). A person who achieves authority in this way is called an *emergent leader*. Note, though, that even in formal groups there are emergent (or 'informal') leaders who exert influence among their peers by virtue of their personal qualities, especially how verbal they are.

Even with appointed leaders, leadership is a complex social process involving an exchange (or transaction) between group members. The leader is dependent on the group members for liking and approval, and their attitudes towards the leader will influence the leadership process. It is easy to overlook the fact that leaders are actually members of the groups they lead. At one and the same time, they represent and embody the group's norms and also act as agents of change, steering the group in new directions. A leader, then, is both a *conformist* (because he or she embodies the group's norms) and a *deviant* (because he or she can change prevailing norms).

However, the right to bring about change must be 'earned' by building up what Hollander (1958) calls *idiosyncrasy credit*. This can be earned by initially conforming closely to established norms, showing the necessary competence to fulfil the group's objectives, identifying with the group's ideals and aspirations, and so on. In one study supportive of this, Merei (1949) brought older children who had previously shown evidence of leadership potential into small groups of younger children in a Hungarian nursery. Merei found that the most successful leaders were those who initially conformed to the existing group practices and gradually introduced minor changes.

Box 3.5 *Two features of a leader's interactions with others*

Whilst the 'leadership as a process' approach is a dynamic one, like Fiedler's it neglects two features of the leader's interactions with others.

- The focus of leadership research has been on the links between leaders and their immediate subordinates. In practice, though, leaders devote substantial time to their own superiors, relevant colleagues, and many others inside (and sometimes outside) the organisations in which they work. According to Likert (1961), leaders play crucial roles as 'linking pins' between various groups within large institutions. This idea has been developed in theories which have reformulated the concept of leadership to emphasise how leader effectiveness can be thought of as the successful management of the conflicting needs and demands of the leader's *role set* (those that make demands on the occupant of a particular role: Smith & Peterson, 1988). Taking this broader view of a leader's interactions implies that the leader uses different leadership styles, or forms of influence, with different members of the role set (Smith, 1995).
- Leaders not only lead their groups but, in varying ways, lead them against other groups. This is illustrated well by the familiar tactic of political leaders who are unpopular at home pursuing aggressive foreign policies. Examples would be Margaret Thatcher's policy in the Falklands conflict (1982) and George Bush's in the Gulf War (1991). This *intergroup dimension* of leadership is usually overlooked in theory and research (Hogg & Vaughan, 1995).

Leadership and power

Clearly, leadership and power are closely related concepts. However, just as there are different kinds of leader (such as appointed and emergent), so there are different kinds of power. One classification of the different types of power was proposed by French & Raven (1959).

Box 3.6   *The five kinds of power identified by French & Raven (1959)*

Legitimate power is the formal power invested in a particular role regardless of the role occupant's personality. Examples of people holding legitimate power include the Prime Minister and a school head teacher.

Reward power refers to control over valued resources (or 'rewards') such as money, food, love, respect and co-operation. Holders of this sort of power include employers, store owners, parents, friends and work colleagues.

Coercive power is the control over feared consequences ('punishments'). Such consequences include the withdrawal of rewards, demotion, loss of love and so on. In both coercive and reward power, power is largely inherent in the role itself, although personality can play some part.

Expert power is the possession of special knowledge, skills and expertise. Holders of this sort of power include doctors, teachers and car mechanics. This is related to *informational power*, which is to do with access to important sources of information such as the Internet.

Referent power consists of personal qualities, such as charm and the ability to persuade and 'win' people over. The *charismatic leader* (Greenberg & Baron, 1995) has great referent power, which often exceeds his or her legitimate power. However, parents, teachers, and so on may also have referent power in addition to their other forms of power.

Possibly, one characteristic consistently displayed by every leader is the *lust after power*. If we accept Adler's (1927) claim that each of us has a 'will to power' (a tendency to overcome our fundamental feelings of inferiority), then perhaps leadership is how leaders satisfy the 'will to power'. According to Gergen & Gergen (1981), however, whilst leadership does imply power, it would be wrong to assume that everybody who possesses power is highly motivated to achieve it. In their view, many political leaders, for example, are recruited and encouraged by others who promote them to powerful positions. If anything, the need for affiliation may be far stronger than the need for power in such people.

Figure 3.2 *Hitler can be regarded as embodying the 'will to power'. His lust for control of Germany's fate influenced the course of world history*

Conclusions

This chapter has reviewed theories concerning the emergence of leaders and the factors that influence leadership effectiveness once a position of power has been attained. Several theoretical positions exist with respect to both leader emergence and leader effectiveness, although the complexity of this area rules out the uncritical acceptance of any one position over any other.

Summary

- A **leader** is the person who exerts most influence in a group. **Leadership** is the exercise of influence or power over others. The **trait approach** to leadership is concerned with whether leaders are born or made. The **situational approach** is concerned with **leader effectiveness**.

- The 'great person' or **trait theory** of leader emergence sees leaders as possessing personality traits which make them suitable for positions of power and authority. However, in general, leaders are not consistently different from non-leaders in terms of their personality traits.

- Another theory stresses the situation's **functional demands**. According to this, the person most likely to emerge as leader is the one whose **skills** and **competence** are most useful to a group in a given setting. This approach assumes that anyone can become a leader in appropriate conditions, although the evidence disputes this.

- Different types of **leadership style** exist. Lewin *et al.* identified **autocratic**, **democratic**, and **laissez-faire styles**, the most favoured being the democratic. **Initiating structure** and **showing consideration** are important behaviours for leaders to exhibit. Other leadership styles are the **task specialist** and **socioemotional specialist**. The most effective leaders display both of these styles.

- Fiedler's **contingency model of leader effectiveness** is mainly concerned with the match between a leader's personal qualities/leadership style and the requirements of the situation in which the group must operate. Fiedler identified **relationship-oriented** and **task-oriented leaders**.

- Fiedler's model proposes that leader effectiveness is contingent upon the fit between the leader's style and a situation's 'favourableness' to the leader. This is determined by the quality of **leader–member relations**, **task structure**, and **position-power**, each of which can have a high or low value.

- The model predicts that a task-oriented leader will be most effective when the situation is either highly favourable or highly unfavourable. A relationship-oriented leader will be more effective when the situation is neither very favourable nor unfavourable.

- Fiedler's predictions have been more strongly supported in laboratory studies than field studies. The model's assumption that leadership style is part of a leader's personality is not, however, supported by evidence. Also, the assumptions regarding the relative importance of the three situational variables is unclear and may be a function of contextual factors.

- **Validation** refers to how a leader achieves **legitimacy** as a leader. In a formal group structure, the leader is **appointed** by an external authority and is imposed on the group. In an informal group, the leader achieves authority from the group members themselves and is an **emergent** leader.

- Even with appointed leaders, leadership is a complex social process involving a transaction between group members. Leaders are also members of the group they lead, and will be influenced by the group. Leaders are simultaneously both conformists (embodying the group's norms) and deviants (capable of changing these norms). Leaders must earn **idiosyncrasy credit** if they are to bring about change.

- This, and Fiedler's approach, overlook the leader's interactions with their own superiors and other relevant colleagues. The view of leaders as 'linking pins' between various groups within large institutions has been adopted by theories which see leader effectiveness in terms of successful management of the leader's role set. This broader view implies that the leader adopts different styles with different members of the role set.

- Five kinds of **power** are **legitimate**, **reward**, **coercive**, **expert** (related to informational power) and **referent** (as displayed by the **charismatic leader**). All leaders may share a 'lust after power'. This could be a way of overcoming a fundamental feeling of inferiority we all experience. However, whilst leadership implies power, not everyone who possesses it is highly motivated to achieve it. Many political leaders have greater needs for affiliation than for power itself.

Introduction and overview

Milgram & Toch (1969) define collective behaviour as:

'behaviour which originates spontaneously, is relatively unorganised, fairly unpredictable and planless in its course of development, and which depends upon interstimulation among participants'.

Several phenomena can be identified as examples of collective behaviour, all of which could be included in this chapter. However, the two types that will be the focus of attention here are *crowds* and *mobs*. This chapter considers explanations and research evidence into these forms of collective behaviour.

Types of collective behaviour

On Milgram and Toch's definition (see above), many phenomena can be identified as examples of collective behaviour.

Box 4.1   *Some examples of collective behaviour*

Panic: Panic is a form of action in which a crowd, excited by a belief in some imminent threat, may engage in uncontrolled, and therefore dangerous, collective flight. The action of the panicky crowd is not wholly irrational. Each individual acts to escape a perceived threat. However, the uncoordinated and uncontrolled action, and the response based on emotional contagion (see page 64), give panic an irrational character.

Fad: A fad is a trivial, short-lived variation in speech, decoration or behaviour. One example of a fad was that for 'streaking', which first emerged in the mid-1970s during the summer months, but died out as winter approached.

Fashion: This is similar to a fad, but is less trivial and changes less rapidly. Long hair in men has been in and out of fashion several times, as have different lengths of women's dresses.

Craze: Whereas a panic is a rush away from a perceived threat, a craze is a rush towards some satisfaction. Crazes differ from fads in that they become obsessions for their followers.

Propaganda: Propaganda includes all efforts to persuade people to a point of view upon an issue. The distinction between education and propaganda is that the former cultivates the ability to make discriminating judgements, whereas the latter seeks to persuade people to the undiscriminating acceptance of a ready-made judgement.

Public opinion: Public opinion can be defined as (1) an opinion held by a substantial number of people, or (2) the dominant opinion among a population. The first use allows for many public opinions, whereas the second refers to public consensus on some issue.

Social movement: A social movement is a 'collectivity' acting with some continuity to promote or resist a change in the society or group of which it is a part.

Revolution: A revolution is a sudden, usually violent, and relatively complete change in a social system.

(Based on Turner & Killian, 1957, Smelser, 1963, and Horton & Hunt, 1976)

Crowds and mobs

Two examples of collective behaviour that could also have appeared in Box 4.1 are crowds and mobs. A *crowd* can be defined as a collection of people gathered around a centre or point of common attention (Young, 1946). Several types of crowd may be distinguished (Brown, 1965). A *casual crowd* is one whose members rarely know one another and whose forms of behaviour are mostly unstructured. In times of social unrest or tension, casual crowds may be transformed into *acting crowds* or *mobs*.

Broom & Selznick (1977) define a mob as:

'a crowd bent upon an aggressive act such as lynching, looting, or the destruction of property. The term refers to a crowd that is fairly unified and single-minded in its aggressive intent. Mob action is not usually randomly destructive but tends to be focused on a single target'.

Box 4.2 *Mob behaviour*

Colonel Charles Lynch provided a name for a particularly barbaric and unofficial method of dealing with crime. Lynch's unofficial courts against those who opposed the revolutionary cause in America in the 1700s did not exact the death penalty. However, they 'filled a gap left by the inadequacies of the official courts' (Sprott, 1958). Two examples of what Cantril (1941) calls *proletariat lynchings*, in which the victim is in a minority and the object is persecution, are those of James Irwin and Arthur Stevens.

- Raper (1933) reports the case of James Irwin, a black man who was chained to a tree in front of around 1000 people. These people watched as members of the mob cut off his fingers and toes joint by joint, pulled out his teeth with wire pliers, castrated him, and 'hung his mangled but living body ... on a tree by the arms'. The mob then set fire to him, and shot him.

- Miller & Dollard (1941) describe the lynching in the southern states of America of a black man called Arthur Stevens. Stevens confessed to murdering his lover, who was white, when she told him she wanted to end their relationship. Because the arresting sheriff feared violence, Stevens was moved 200 miles during the night of his arrest. However, over 100 people stormed the gaol and returned Stevens to the scene of his crime. There, he was tortured, emasculated and murdered. After dragging his body through the town, the mob went on the rampage, chasing and beating other black people. Their behaviour was brought to an end only by the intervention of troops.

Figure 4.1 *The Heysel Stadium football disaster: a casual crowd became an acting crowd or mob*

Theoretical approaches to collective behaviour

Turner & Killian (1972) identify several broad theoretical approaches to collective behaviour which have been specifically applied to crowds and mobs. The three most important of these are *contagion theories, convergence theories*, and *emergent norm theories*.

Contagion theories

According to Le Bon (1897):

> 'isolated, a man may be a cultured individual; in a crowd he is a bar-barian. [Crowd behaviour is] an irrational and uncritical response to the psychological temptations of the crowd situation'.

In Le Bon's view, the question that needed answering was why crowds act in ways that are uncharacteristic of the individuals comprising them and in ways contrary to their everyday norms. Le Bon identified several situational determinants of behaviour which come into operation when a crowd is assembled, these being *suggestibility, social contagion, impersonality* and *anonymity*. The last of these has been the subject of most research.

Suggestibility

In the absence of a leader or recognised behaviour patterns for members of a crowd to carry out, a situation may be chaotic and confused. Suggestion, if made in an authoritative manner, may lead people to react readily and uncritically (Lang & Lang, 1961). Le Bon believed that, in such circumstances, what he called the 'conscious personality' vanished, and the 'racial unconscious' took over.

Whilst few psychologists today would agree with this view, Freud (1921) suggested that crowds permit the expression of behaviour that would otherwise be *repressed*. According to Freud, we possess a need, derived from our relationship with our father, to submit to more powerful forces, whether embodied in authorities or groups. Whilst some (e.g. Couch, 1968) believe that the role played by suggestibility has been overemphasised, heightened suggestibility does make *rumour* an important part of collective behaviour.

Box 4.3   *Rumour*

According to Shibutani (1966), heightened suggestibility makes rumour important in situations of collective excitement. A rumour is an unconfirmed, but not necessarily false, communication. Usually it is transmitted by word of mouth in a situation of anxiety or stress. Rumours occur in unstructured situations when information is needed but reliable channels do not exist.

Rumours tend to be passed rapidly from person to person and usually distort or falsify the facts. This is because they are often coloured by emotions. A rumour may begin as an inaccurate report because of the narrowing of perception that occurs in emotionally charged situations. It may become progressively more distorted because *all* oral communication is subject to distortion. Even in the absence of emotional elements, factual reports tend to become shorter and simpler as they are passed on. The distortion of details typically occurs in accordance with personal or cultural predispositions or 'sets'. This relates to Bartlett's theory of reconstructive memory (see Gross & McIlveen, 1998).
(Adapted from Broom & Selznick, 1977)

Social contagion

Social contagion (or *interactional amplification*) is the process whereby the members of a crowd stimulate and respond to one another and thereby increase their emotional intensity and responsiveness (Horton & Hunt, 1976). When so aroused, a crowd needs emotional release, and it may act on the first suggested action which accords with its impulses (Lang & Lang, 1961). Thus, when an intended black victim of a lynching was protected by the town's mayor, the mob attempted to lynch the mayor and very nearly succeeded (Horton & Hunt, 1976).

Impersonality

Consider the account of a shooting reported by Lee & Humphrey (1943) described below.

Box 4.4 *An impersonal attack*

We drove around for a long time. We saw a lot of coloured people, but they were in bunches. We didn't want any of that. We wanted some guy all by himself. We saw one at Mack Avenue.

Aldo drove past him and then said 'Gimme that gun'. I handed it over to him and he turned around and came back. We were about 15 feet from the man when Aldo pulled up, almost stopped and shot. The man fell and we blew.

We didn't know him. He wasn't bothering us. But other people were fighting and killing and we felt like it, too.

(From Lee & Humphrey, 1943)

The description given above shows *impersonality*. In the case of a *riot* (see page 74), the impersonality of crowd behaviour is illustrated by treating one member of the 'enemy' as being as bad as another (which explains why innocent passersby are often the victims of a riot).

Anonymity

Le Bon believed that the more anonymous the crowd, the greater was its potential for extreme action, because anonymity removes the sense of *individuality* from members. When a person does not feel that he or she is being singled out as an individual, and when attention is not paid to others as individuals, restraints on behaviour are removed and a person is 'free' to indulge in behaviour that would ordinarily be controlled. The reason for this is that moral responsibility for behaviour has been shifted from the individual person to the group of which he or she is a member.

As mentioned earlier (see page 63), Le Bon wanted to know why people in crowds act in uncharacteristic ways and contrary to their everyday norms. Fromm (1941), however, was more concerned with the *motives* that lead some people to hide their individuality in crowds. Le Bon and Fromm's concerns were combined by Festinger *et al.* (1952), who proposed the concept of *deindividuation*, defining it as:

> 'a state of affairs in a group where members do not pay attention to other individuals qua individuals and, correspondingly, the members do not feel they are being singled out by others'.

According to Festinger *et al.*, membership of a group not only provides us with a sense of identity and *belongingness*, but allows us to merge with the group, forego our individualities, and become anonymous. This may lead to a reduction of inner constraints and inhibitions. A field experiment demonstrating the effects of anonymity was reported by Zimbardo (1969). Zimbardo reasoned that a big city is a more anonymous place than a small town, because people are more likely to know one another in a small town. For the big city, the Bronx area of New York was chosen. The little town was the Stanford area of Palo Alto, California.

In each location, a similar car was parked in a street adjoining a university campus. The car's number plates were removed and its bonnet raised in order to make it appear that it had been abandoned. Research assistants photographed the car and filmed people's behaviour from hidden locations. In New York, the car's battery and radiator were removed within ten minutes of it being parked. Within a day, just about everything else that could be removed was. Within three days, there was little left of the car, a result of 23 incidents of 'destructive contact'. These were nearly always observed by a passerby, who occasionally stopped to chat with the perpetrator. Moreover, the incidents were carried out in daylight by well-dressed, clean-cut whites who, argued Zimbardo, were the very people who would protest against such behaviour and demand a greater police presence! By contrast, the car left in Palo Alto was left alone for seven days. Indeed, on the day it rained, a passer-by lowered the car's bonnet in order to protect its engine!

Box 4.5 *Some research showing the effects of deindividuation*

- Defining deindividuation as 'a subjective state in which people lose their sense of self-consciousness', Singer *et al.* (1965) found that reduced individuality within a group was associated with a greater liking for the group and a larger number of obscene comments being made in a discussion of pornography. In a follow-up study, Singer *et al.* found that although deindividuated participants liked their group more, they conformed to it less.

- In one of several studies conducted by Zimbardo (1969), female undergraduates were required to deliver electric shocks to another student as 'an aid to learning'. Half the participants wore bulky laboratory coats and hoods that hid their faces. These participants were spoken to in groups of four and never referred to by name. The other half wore their normal clothes, were given large name tags to wear, and introduced to each other by name. They could also see each other dimly whilst giving the shocks.

  Both sets of participants could see the student supposedly receiving the shocks, who pretended to be in extreme discomfort. The hooded participants gave twice as much shock as the other group. Moreover, the amount of shock given by the hooded participants, unlike that given by the other group, did not depend on whether they were told that the student receiving the shocks was 'honest, sincere and warm' or 'conceited and critical'.

- Watson (1973) investigated 23 different cultures. Those warriors who depersonalised themselves with face paints or masks were significantly more likely than those with exposed faces to kill, torture or mutilate captured enemies.

- Diener *et al.* (1976) observed 1300 'trick-or-treating' American children one Halloween night. When the children were anonymous, as a result of wearing costumes which prevented them from being recognised, and went from house to house in large groups, they were more likely to steal money and candy.

Diener's theory of deindividuation

According to Diener (1980):

'a deindividuated person is prevented by situational factors in a group from becoming self-aware. Deindividuated persons are

blocked from an awareness of themselves as separate individuals and from monitoring their own behaviour'.

Diener argues that in everyday life we are frequently unaware of our individual identities or of ourselves as separate persons. Indeed, when we perform well-learned behaviours, express well-thought-out cognitions, or enact culturally scripted behaviour, we are not consciously aware. In some circumstances, such as when we are evaluated by others or when a behaviour does not produce an expected outcome, self-awareness and behavioural self-regulation are initiated. In other circumstances, such as when we are immersed in a group, self-awareness and individual self-conception are blocked, and it is this which Diener believes leads to deindividuation. When deindividuation occurs, certain self-regulatory capacities are lost. These include a weakening of normal restraints against impulsive behaviour, a lack of concern about what others will think of our behaviour, and a reduced capability to engage in rational thinking.

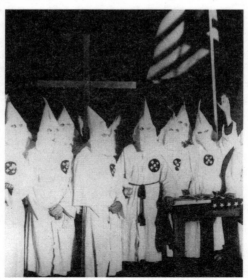

Figure 4.2 *The Ku Klux Klan: deindividuated individuals but an easily identifiable group*

Prentice-Dunn and Rogers' theory of deindividuation

Prentice-Dunn & Rogers (1983) argue that it is possible to distinguish between two types of self-awareness. *Public self-awareness* refers to a concern about the impression we are giving others who will hold us accountable for our behaviour. *Private self-awareness* refers to the attention we pay our own thoughts and feelings.

Public self-awareness can be reduced by three factors. For example, we would be difficult to identify in a crowd and this would make us feel *anonymous*. If other members were behaving anti-socially, a *diffusion of responsibility* would also occur because one person alone could not be blamed for the group's actions. Finally, other group members' behaviours would set some sort of standard or *norm* for behaviour and supply models to *imitate* (see also emergent norm theory: page 73).

Private self-awareness can also be reduced by several factors. For example, in a crowd attending a rock concert, our attention would be directed outward, and we might become so engrossed in what was going on (singing, dancing, and/or drinking alcohol, for example) that we would 'forget' who we are. Prentice-Dunn and Rogers argue that deviant behaviour can occur through a loss of either of these forms of self-awareness, although this occurs through different routes.

When we are publicly self-aware, we engage in rational calculations about the likelihood of being punished for deviant behaviour. A deindividuated state, however, is an *irrational state of altered consciousness*. As Figure 4.3 (see page 70) illustrates, Prentice-Dunn and Rogers' theory does not see reductions in public or private self-awareness by themselves as causing deviant behaviour. Rather, both factors make us susceptible to *behavioural cues*, one being other people's behaviour in a crowd.

The data presented in Box 4.5 (page 67) are consistent with both theories described above. These theories may also explain other phenomena such as the 'baiting crowd' in cases of threatened suicide. For example, in an analysis of 21 incidents of

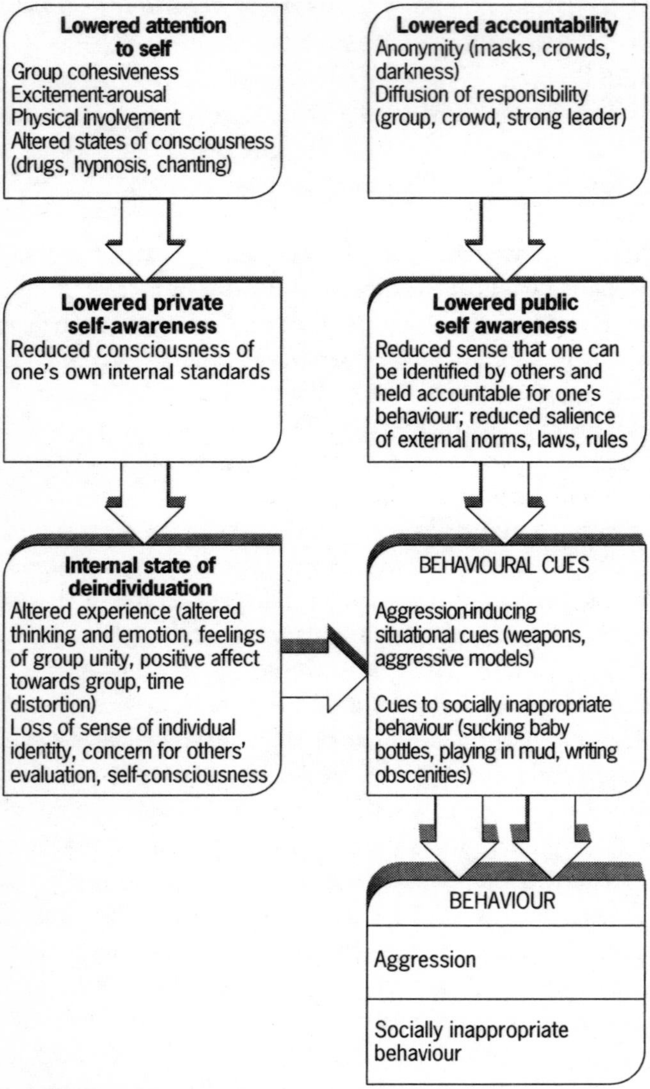

Figure 4.3 *Prentice-Dunn and Roger's theory sees deviant behaviour as occurring through two different paths, namely lowered attention to self and lowered accountability (From Prentice-Dunn & Rogers, 1983)*

potential suicides threatening to jump from buildings, Mann (1981) found that in ten cases, people were more likely to shout 'Jump!' when they were part of a large crowd, when it was dark, and when the victim and crowd were distant from one another (as is the case when the victim threatens to jump from a tall building). Baiting was also linked to other behavioural cues (see above), such as high temperatures and how long the episode lasted.

An evaluation of deindividuation research

Although there is much experimental support for the concept of deindividuation, several cautions should be exercised. First, participants in Zimbardo's (1969) study outlined in Box 4.5 wore clothing resembling that worn by the Ku Klux Klan, an American racist group (see Figure 4.2). This uniform may have acted as a *demand characteristic*, in that it might have led American participants to believe that more extreme behaviour was expected of them (Johnson & Downing, 1979). In support of this, Johnson and Downing found that when participants wore surgical masks and gowns, they delivered significantly *less* electric shock than those participants whose names and identities were emphasised. This suggests that the participants' clothing, rather than deindividuation, may have led to differences in behaviour. Similarly, Brown (1985) has pointed out that in another of Zimbardo's (1969) studies, the participants were Belgian soldiers rather than the female undergraduates investigated in the study described in Box 4.5. When these soldiers wore the hoods, they did *not* behave more aggressively. Instead, they became self-conscious, suspicious and anxious. Their apparently *individuated* counterparts, who wore army-issue uniform, retained their 'normal' level of deindividuation, resulting from their status as *uniformed soldiers*. One of the functions of uniforms in the 'real world' is to reduce individuality and hence, at least indirectly, to increase deindividuation (Brown, 1985). Indeed, dispossessing someone of the clothes they normally wear is a major technique of depersonalising them in 'total institutions', such as prisons and psychiatric hospitals (Goffman, 1968, 1971).

Also, whilst the anonymity produced by wearing, say, police or military uniform may increase the likelihood of deindividuated behaviour, such anonymity may make the wearers of these uniforms appear less human and affect the perceptions and attitudes of others (Brown, 1985).

Box 4.6 *Do crowds resent the anonymity of their opponents?*

In a disturbance in the Notting Hill area of London in 1982, 100 police officers were sent to the scene wearing special flameproof suits. According to *The Times* newspaper:

(The) uniform, combined with a hard helmet and visor, does not include a police serial number, making it difficult for anyone who wishes to identify and complain against an individual officer to pursue a grievance. A middle-aged West Indian, who was in a restaurant when it was raided, said yesterday: 'When they came through the door they looked like zombies, dressed in full black with headgear. All they had was one white stripe saying 'police' on it. We could not know in the world who they were, their faces were covered and they had helmets.'

(Taken from Brown, 1985)

Finally, deindividuation does not necessarily produce anti-social behaviour. Gergen *et al.* (1973) showed that in some circumstances when people cannot be identified, more *affiliative* behaviours can occur. In their study, groups of six men and six women were placed in either a normally lit room (control group) or a completely dark room (experimental group). The participants, who had never met one another, were told that there was nothing special the experimenters wanted them to do. The experimenters left the participants for one hour, tape recorded what they said and, when the experiment was over, asked them what had happened.

During the first 15 minutes, the experimental group participants mainly explored the room and chatted idly to one another.

In the following 30 minutes, the conversation turned to more serious matters. In the final 15 minutes, the participants began to get physical in that half of them hugged one another. Some of them became quite intimate, and 80 per cent reported feeling sexually aroused! It seems that we can become uninhibited in the dark where the norms of intimacy no longer prevail. We feel less accountable for our behaviour in such situations, but this state of deindividuation can be to the mutual benefit of all (Gergen & Gergen, 1981).

Convergence theory

Convergence theory (e.g. Shellow & Roemer, 1966) argues that crowd behaviour arises from the gathering together of people who share the same needs, impulses, dislikes and purposes. According to Durkheim (1898), 'controlled emotional contagion' (as occurs in a peaceful crowd) can serve a useful social function. For example, it may allow people to release emotions and tensions they cannot ordinarily express (consider, for instance, the behaviour of some types of spectators at wrestling bouts) and stimulate feelings that enhance group solidarity.

Organised gatherings of many kinds (such as mass meetings and religious services) provide settings that integrate crowd behaviour into the social structure (Broom & Selznick, 1977). For example, Benewick & Holton (1987) interviewed members of the 80,000-strong crowd that gathered at Wembley Stadium for an open air-mass given by the Pope during his visit to Britain in 1982. Interviewees reported that they found the event powerful and meaningful, and experienced strong feelings of unity with the others present.

Emergent norm theory

One weakness of contagion theory is that it does not explain why a crowd takes one course of action rather than another (Turner & Killian, 1957; Turner, 1964). According to emergent norm theorists, contagion theorists are guilty of exaggerating the irrational and purposeless components of crowd behaviour. In support of this, consider social psychological analyses of certain *riots*.

Smelser (1963) defines a riot as a form of civil disorder marked by violent mob action, a 'hostile outburst' of resentment or rebelliousness. Prior to the 1960s, the dominant view of riots was the *riffraff theory*. As applied to race riots, this says that the small percentage of people who take part in riots are criminals, drug addicts, drifters, leaders of youth gangs, and welfare cheaters, and that a riot is an isolated event which receives little or no support from the community (Sears & McConahay, 1969).

Analyses conducted in the 1960s, however, showed that there was little if any truth in riffraff theory. For example, Orum (1972) found that participants in American race riots were relatively representative cross-sections of the categories of people involved. Moreover, they were motivated by genuine group grievances rather than personal instabilities.

Orum found that the burning and looting which accompanied race riots was *not* indiscriminate. Whilst stores and offices perceived as exploitative were looted and burned, private homes, public buildings, and agencies serving the needs of the people were usually spared. Of course, not all riots are alike, but according to emergent norm theory the perceptions and grievances of a group, fed by the contagion process, lead to the emergence of a norm which justifies and sets limits to the behaviour of the crowd (Horton & Hunt, 1976).

An analysis of why 'ordinary people' can turn into looters and rioters was attempted by Brown (1954). According to Brown, there are varying *thresholds for participation* in physical action.

Box 4.7 *Brown's thresholds for participation*

1 **The lawless:** These are impulsive people, usually men and often with criminal records, who need little provocation before they try to retaliate. The lawless have little understanding of or concern for the consequences of their actions.

2 **The suggestible:** These are people who are easily influenced by an impulsive leader. They only need 'a little push' to follow an example, although it is unlikely that they would initiate action on their own.

3 **The cautious:** These are people with strong interests in the kinds of action initiated by others, but who would not act because of a fear of the law. If this constraint is lifted, they take action in pursuit of their own interests.

4 **The yielders:** These are people who are easily persuaded that everybody is engaged in a particular behaviour. Yielders act when a sufficient number of people are acting because they do not want to be left out, and see an action as right because others are engaged in it.

5 **The supportive:** Whilst the supportive cannot be 'stampeded' into action, they do not actively oppose it. They may watch or shout encouragement. They are not violent, but they do not stand out against violence in others.

6 **The resisters:** These are people whose values are opposed to mob action, and who will not support it even passively. Because of this, they are in danger of their lives if they speak up at the wrong time.

(Based on Brown, 1954)

In an extension of emergent norm theory, Reicher (1984) has proposed a model of collective behaviour based on *social identity*. Reicher argues that a crowd is:

'a form of social group in the sense of a set of individuals who perceive themselves as members of a common *social* category, or, to put it another way, adopt a common social identification'.

Reicher analysed the riots that occurred in the St Paul's area of Bristol in 1980. Following a tip-off about illegal drinking, police raided a cafe and arrested two men. However, as they tried to leave, bricks were thrown at them. Police reinforcements subsequently arrived, and were attacked by a crowd of several thousand who overturned cars and set them alight.

Reicher's analysis showed that the crowd did not behave in a random and unpredictable manner. For example, they did not damage any vehicles other than police cars and those suspected of being unmarked police cars, and did minimal damage to property. The crowd also confined its behaviour to the St Paul's district and prevented any other forms of violence from taking place. In Reicher's view, the crowd saw the police as an illegitimate presence. The community members (the *ingroup*) behaved in a way they perceived as being legitimate given the police's presence.

Unfortunately, Reicher's analysis is weakened by the finding that crowds do not always behave in a like-minded way. During the riot that took place in the Watts district of Los Angeles, looting and burning occurred at different times and in different areas. Whether these actions, occurring in different locations and at varying times, are the expression of common social identity is difficult to answer without considerable first-hand experience of riots (Brown, 1985).

Conclusions

This chapter has reviewed explanations and evidence concerning crowds and mobs, two important examples of collective behaviour. Several theoretical accounts have been advanced to explain their behaviour. However, whilst supported to some extent by evidence, none offers a completely adequate account of such behaviour.

Summary

- Two extensively researched examples of collective behaviour are **crowds** and **mobs**. A crowd is a collection of people gathered around some point of common attention. **Casual**

crowds can be transformed into **acting crowds** or **mobs** at times of social unrest. A mob is a crowd bent upon an aggressive act such as lynching, looting, or the destruction of property. A mob is fairly unified and single-minded in its aggressive intent, and tends to be focused on a single target (as in **proletariat lynchings**).

- The three most important theoretical approaches to collective behaviour which apply specifically to crowds and mobs are **contagion**, **convergence** and **emergent norm theories**.

- Le Bon's version of contagion theory tried to explain why crowds behave in ways uncharacteristic of the individuals composing them and contrary to everyday norms. He identified several situational influences on crowd behaviour, namely **suggestibility** (and **rumour**), **social contagion** (**interactional amplification**), **impersonality**, and **anonymity**.

- The more anonymous the crowd, the greater its potential for extreme action, since members lose their sense of **individuality**. This, combined with a failure to perceive others as individuals, removes restraints on behaviour, freeing the person to indulge in behaviour that is ordinarily controlled. Moral responsibility is shifted from the individual to the group.

- Through the concept of **deindividuation**, Festinger *et al.* combined Fromm's concerns with people's motives for hiding individuality with Le Bon's concern for people's uncharacteristic behaviours in crowds. Groups provide us with a sense of identity and belongingness and an opportunity to merge in with them, thus foregoing our individuality and becoming anonymous. This may reduce our inner constraints and inhibitions.

- According to Diener, **deindividuated** people are prevented from forming an awareness of themselves as separate individuals and from monitoring their own behaviours. This occurs when immersed in a group, resulting in certain self-regulatory capacities being lost.

- Prentice-Dunn and Rogers distinguish between **public** and **private self-awareness**, both of which can be reduced by being in a crowd. Deviant behaviour can occur through a loss of either type of self-awareness. However, this happens indirectly, either through inducing an internal state of deindividuation (an **irrational state of altered consciousness**) in the case of reduced private self-awareness, or making us more susceptible to **behavioural cues** (such as other people's behaviour in a crowd) in the case of reduced public self-awareness.

- There is considerable experimental support for the concept of deindividuation, although some findings are open to alternative explanations. Additionally, under some circumstances, deindividuation can increase affiliative behaviours.

- According to **convergence theory**, crowd behaviour is the result of the gathering of people sharing the same needs, impulses, dislikes and goals. 'Controlled emotional contagion' can be socially useful, as when people release tension at a sporting event, or when group solidarity is increased. Many organised gatherings provide settings that integrate crowd behaviour into the social structure.

- **Emergent norm theory** argues that contagion theories overemphasise the irrational and purposeless components of crowd behaviour. In **riots**, for example, people are motivated by genuine group grievances. Whilst not all riots are alike, emergent norm theory claims that a group's perceptions and grievances, fed by contagion, lead to the emergence of a norm which justifies and sets limits to the crowd's behaviour.

- In Reicher's extension of emergent norm theory, a crowd is seen as a set of individuals who adopt a common **social identity**. The crowd involved in the St Paul's riots in Bristol did not behave randomly and unpredictably but in a way it perceived as legitimate. However, Reicher's view is weakened by those riots in which looting and burning occur at different locations at varying times.

REFERENCES

ABRAMS, D., WETHERELL, M., COCHRANE, S., HOGG, M.A. & TURNER, J.C. (1990) Knowing what to think by knowing who you are: Self-categorization and the nature of norm formation. *British Journal of Social Psychology*, 29, 97–119.

ADLER, A. (1927) *The Practice and Theory of Individual Psychology*. New York: Harcourt Brace Jovanovich.

ALLEN, V.L. & LEVINE, J.M. (1971) Social support and conformity: The role of independent assessment of reality. *Journal of Experimental Social Psychology*, 7, 48–58.

ANCONA, L. & PAREYSON, R. (1968) Contributo allo studio della a aggressione: la dinimica della obbedienza distructiva. *Archivio di Psichologia Neurologia e Psichiatria*, 29, 340–372.

ARENDT, H. (1965) *Eichmann in Jerusalem: A Report on the Banality of Evil*. New York: Viking.

ARONSON, E. (1988) *The Social Animal* (5th edition). New York: Freeman.

ASCH, S.E. (1951) Effect of group pressure upon the modification and distortion of judgements. In H. Guetzkow (Ed.) *Groups, Leadership and Men*. Pittsburgh, PA: Carnegie Press.

ASCH, S.E. (1952) *Social Psychology*. Englewood Cliffs, NJ: Prentice Hall.

ASCH, S.E. (1955) Opinions and social pressure. *Scientific American*, 193, 31–35.

ASCH, S.E. (1956) Studies of independence and submission to group pressure: 1: A minority of one against a unanimous majority. *Psychological Monographs*, 70, Whole No. 416.

BALES, R.F. (1950) *Interactional Process Analysis: A Method for the Study of Small Groups*. Reading, MA: Addison Wesley.

BALES, R.F. & SLATER, P. (1955) Role differentiation in small decision-making groups. In T. Parsons & R.F. Bales (Eds) *Family, Socialisation and Interaction Processes*. New York: Free Press.

BAUMRIND, D. (1964) Some thoughts on the ethics of research: After reading Milgram's behavioural study of obedience. *American Psychologist*, 19, 421–423.

BENEWICK, R. & HOLTON, R. (1987) The peaceful crowd: Crowd solidarity and the Pope's visit to Britain. In G. Gaskell & R. Benewick (Eds) *The Crowd in Contemporary Britain*. London: Sage.

BERKOWITZ, L. (1986) *A Survey of Social Psychology* (3rd edition). New York: Holt, Rinehart & Winston.

BERKOWITZ, L. (1993) *Aggression: Its Causes, Consequences and Control*. New York: McGraw-Hill.

BICKMAN, L. (1974) The social power of a uniform. *Journal of Applied Social Psychology*, 1, 47–61.

BOGDONOFF, M.D., KLEIN, R.F., ESTES, E.H., SHAW, D.M. & BACK, K. (1961) The modifying effect of conforming behaviour upon lipid responses accompanying CNS arousal. *Clinical Research*, 9, 135.

BREHM, J.W. (1966) *A Theory of Psychological Reactance*. New York: Academic Press.

BROOM, L. & SELZNICK, P. (1977) *Sociology* (6th edition). London: Harper & Row.

BROWN, H. (1985) *People, Groups and Society*. Milton Keynes: Open University Press.

BROWN, R. (1954) Mass phenomena. In G. Lindzey (Ed.) *Handbook of Social Psychology*. London: Addison-Wesley.

BROWN, R. (1965) *Social Psychology*. New York: The Free Press.

BROWN, R. (1986) *Social Psychology: The Second Edition*. New York: Free Press.

BROWN, R.J. (1988) Intergroup relations. In M. Hewstone, W. Stroebe, J.P. Codol & G.M. Stephenson (Eds) *Introduction to Social Psychology*. Oxford: Blackwell.

CANTRIL, H. (1941) *The Psychology of Social Movements*. New York: Wiley.

CARLSON, N.R. (1987) *Discovering Psychology*. London: Allyn & Bacon.

CLARK, R.D. & MAASS, A. (1988) The role of social categorization and perceived source credibility in minority influence. *European Journal of Social Psychology*, 18, 381–394.

COLMAN, A.M. (1987) *Facts, Fallacies and Frauds in Psychology*. London: Unwin Hyman.

COOPER, H.M. (1979) Statistically combining independent studies: A meta-analysis of sex differences in conformity research. *Journal of Personality and Social Psychology*, 37, 131–146.

COSTANTINI, E. & CRAIK, K.H. (1980) Personality and politicians: California party leaders, 1960–1976. *Journal of Personality and Social Psychology*, 38, 641–661.

COUCH, C.J. (1968) Collective behaviour: An examination of some stereotypes. *Social Problems*, 15, 310–322.

CRIDER, A.B., GOETHALS, G.R., KAVANAUGH, R.D. & SOLOMON, P.R. (1989) *Psychology* (3rd edition). London: Scott, Foresman and Company.

CRUTCHFIELD, R.S. (1954) A new technique for measuring individual differences in conformity to group judgement. *Proceedings of the Invitational Conference on Testing Problems*, 69–74.

CRUTCHFIELD, R.S. (1955) Conformity and character. *American Psychologist*, 10, 191–198.

DEUTSCH, M. & GERARD, H.B. (1955) A study of normative and informational social influence upon individual judgement. *Journal of Abnormal and Social Psychology*, 51, 629–636.

DIENER, E. (1980) Deindividuation: The absence of self-awareness and self-regulation in group members. In P.B. Paulus (Ed.) *Psychology of Group Influence*. Hillsdale, NJ: Erlbaum.

DIENER, E., FRASER, S.C., BEAMAN, A.L. & KELEM, R.T. (1976) Effects of deindividuation variables on stealing among Halloween trick-or-treaters. *Journal of Personality and Social Psychology*, 33, 178–183.

DURKHEIM, E. (1898) Représentations individuelles et représentations collectives. *Revue de Métaphysique et de Morale*, 6. 273–302.

EAGLY, A.H. & STEFFEN, V.J. (1984) Gender stereotypes stem from the distribution of men and women into social roles. *Journal of Personality and Social Psychology*, 46, 735–754.

FESTINGER, L. (1954) A theory of social comparison processes. *Human Relations*, 7, 117–140.

FESTINGER, L., PEPITONE, A. & NEWCOMB, T. (1952) Some consequences of deindividuation in a group. *Journal of Abnormal and Social Psychology*, 47, 382–389.

FIEDLER, F.E. (1964) A contingency model of leadership effectiveness. In L. Berkowitz (Ed.) *Group Processes*. New York: Academic Press.

FIEDLER, F.E. (1967) *A Theory of Leadership Effectiveness*. New York: McGraw-Hill.

FIEDLER, F.E. (1981) Leadership effectiveness. *American Behavioural Scientist*, 24, 619–632.

FIEDLER, F.E. & CHEMERS, M. (1984) *Improving Leadership Effectiveness: The Leader Match Concept*. New York: Wiley.

FRENCH, J.R.P. & RAVEN, B.H. (1959) The bases of social power. In D. Cartwright (Ed.) *Studies in Social Power*. Ann Arbour, MI: Institute for Social Research, University of Michigan.

FREUD, S. (1921) *Group Psychology and the Analysis of the Ego. (Standard Edition,* Volume 18*)*. London: The Hogarth Press (1955).

FROMM, E. (1941) *Escape From Freedom*. New York: Farrar & Rinehart.

GAMSON, W.B., FIREMAN, B. & RYTINA, S. (1982) *Encounters with Unjust Authority.* Hounwood, IL: Dorsey Press.

GERGEN, K.J. & GERGEN, M.M. (1981) *Social Psychology.* New York: Harcourt Brace Jovanovich,

GERGEN, K.J., GERGEN, M.M. & BARTON, W. (1973) Deviance in the dark. *Psychology Today*, 7, 129–130.

GILBERT, S.J. (1981) Another look at the Milgram obedience studies: The role of the graduated series of shocks. *Personality and Social Psychology Bulletin*, 7, 690–695.

GOFFMAN, E. (1968) *Asylums – Essay on the Social Situation of Mental Patients and Other Inmates.* Harmondsworth: Penguin.

GOFFMAN, E. (1971) *The Presentation of Self in Everyday Life.* Harmondsworth: Penguin.

GREENBERG, J. & BARON, R.A. (1995) *Behaviour in Organisations.* London: Prentice-Hall.

GROSS, R. (1996) *Psychology: The Science of Mind and Behaviour.* (3rd edition) London: Hodder & Stoughton.

GROSS, R. & McILVEEN, R. (1998) *Psychology: A New Introduction.* London: Hodder & Stoughton.

HALPIN, A. & WINER, B. (1952) *The Leadership Behaviour of the Airplane Commander.* Columbus, OH: Ohio State University Research Foundation.

HAMILTON, V.L. (1978) Obedience and responsibility: A jury simulation. *Journal of Personality and Social Psychology*, 36, 126–146.

HIRSCH, H. (1995) *Genocide and the Politics of Memory.* Chapel Hill, NC: The University of North Carolina Press.

HOFLING, K.C., BROTZMAN, E., DALRYMPLE, S., GRAVES, N. & PIERCE, C.M. (1966) An experimental study in the nurse–physician relationships. *Journal of Nervous and Mental Disorders*, 143, 171–180.

HOGG, M.A. & VAUGHAN, G.M. (1995) *Social Psychology: An Introduction.* Hemel Hempstead: Prentice Hall/Harvester Wheatsheaf.

HOLLANDER, E.P. (1958) Conformity, status, and idiosyncracy credit. *Psychological Review*, 65, 117–127.

HOLLANDER, E.P. (1985) Leadership and power. In G. Lindsay & E. Aronson (Eds) *Handbook of Social Psychology* (3rd edition). New York: Random House.

HORTON, P.B. & HUNT, C.L. (1976) *Sociology* (4th edition). New York: McGraw-Hill.

HUCZYNSKI, A. & BUCHANAN, D. (1991) *Organisational Behaviour: An Introductory Text* (2nd edition). Hemel Hempstead: Prentice-Hall.

HUMPHREYS, P.W. (1994) Obedience after Milgram. *Psychology Review*, 1, 2–5.

INSKO, C.A., DRENAN, S., SOLOMON, M.R., SMITH, R. & WADE, T.J. (1983) Conformity as a function of the consistency of positive self-evaluation with being liked and being right. *Journal of Experimental Social Psychology*, 19, 341–358.

JOHNSON, R.D. & DOWNING, L.E. (1979) Deindividuation and valence of cues: Effects on prosocial and antisocial behaviour. *Journal of Personality and Social Psychology*, 37, 1532–1538.

KELMAN, H. & LAWRENCE, L. (1972) Assignment of responsibility in the case of Lt. Calley: Preliminary report on a national survey. *Journal of Social Issues*, 28, 177–212.

KILHAM, W. & MANN, L. (1974) Level of destructive obedience as a function of transmitter and executant roles in the Milgram obedience paradigm. *Journal of Personality and Social Psychology*, 29, 696–702.

KIRKPATRICK, S.A. & LOCKE, E.A. (1991) Leadership: Do traits matter? *Academy of Management Executives*, 5, 48–60.

KREBS, D. & BLACKMAN, R. (1988) *Psychology: A First Encounter*. New York: Harcourt Brace Jovanovich.

LANG, K. & LANG, G.E. (1961) *Collective Dynamics*. New York: Thomas Y. Crowell Co.

LARSEN, K.S. (1974) Conformity in the Asch experiment. *Journal of Social Psychology*, 94, 303–304.

LARSEN, K.S., TRIPLETT, J.S., BRANT, W.D. & LANGENBERG, D. (1979) Collaborator status, subject characteristics and conformity in the Asch paradigm. *Journal of Social Psychology*, 108, 259–263.

LE BON, G. (1897) *The Crowd: A Study of the Popular Mind*. London: Unwin.

LEE, A.M. & HUMPHREY, N.D. (1943) *Race Riot*. New York: Holt, Rinehart & Winston.

LEWIN, K., LIPPITT, R. & WHITE, R. (1939) Patterns of aggressive behaviour in experimentally created 'social climates'. *Journal of Social Psychology*, 10, 271–299.

LIKERT, R. (1961) *New Patterns of Management*. New York: McGraw-Hill.

MANN, L. (1969) *Social Psychology*. New York: Wiley.

MANN, L. (1981) The baiting crowd in episodes of threatened suicide. *Journal of Personality and Social Psychology*, 41, 703–709.

MASLACH, C., STAPP, J. & SANTEE, R.T. (1985) Individuation: Conceptual analysis and assessment. *Journal of Personality and Social Psychology*, 49, 729–738.

MEEUS, W.H.J & RAAIJMAKERS, Q.A.W. (1986) Administrative obedience: Carrying out orders to use psychological-administrative violence. *European Journal of Social Psychology*, 16, 311–324.

MEREI, F. (1949) Group leadership and institutionalisation. *Human Relations*, 2, 18–30.

MILGRAM, S. (1963) Behavioural study of obedience. *Journal of Abnormal and Social Psychology*, 67, 391–398.

MILGRAM, S. (1964) Issues in the study of obedience: A reply to Baumrind. *American Psychologist*, 19, 848–852.

MILGRAM, S. (1965) Liberating effects of group pressure. *Journal of Personality and Social Psychology*, 1, 127–134.

MILGRAM, S. (1974) *Obedience to Authority*. New York: Harper & Row.

MILGRAM, S. (1992) *The Individual in a Social World* (2nd edition). New York: McGraw-Hill.

MILGRAM, S. & TOCH, H. (1969) Collective behaviour: Crowds and social movements. In G. Lindzey & E. Aronson (Eds) *Handbook of Social Psychology*, Volume 4. Reading, MA: Addison-Wesley.

MILLER, N.E. & DOLLARD, J. (1941) *Social Learning and Imitation*. New Haven, CT.: Yale University Press.

MOSCOVICI, S. (1976) *La Psychoanalyse: Son Image et Son Public* (2nd edition). Paris: Presses Universitaires de France.

MOSCOVICI, S. & FAUCHEUX, C. (1972) Social influence, conforming bias and the study of active minorities. In L. Berkowitz (Ed.) *Advances in Experimental Social Psychology*, Volume 6. New York: Academic Press.

MOSCOVICI, S. & LAGE, E. (1976) Studies in social influence III: Majority versus minority influence in a group. *European Journal of Social Psychology*, 6, 149–174.

MULLEN, B. (1983) Operationalising the effect of the group on the individual: A self-attentive perspective. *Journal of Experimental Social Psychology*, 19, 295–322.

NEMETH, C. & WACHTLER, J. (1973) Consistency and modification of judgement. *Journal of Experimental Social Psychology*, 9, 65–79.

NYDEGGER, R.V. (1975) Information processing complexity and leadership status. *Journal of Experimental Social Psychology*, 11, 317–328.

OPTON, E.M. (1973) 'It never happened and besides they deserved it.' In W.E. Henry & N. Sanford (Eds) *Sanctions for Evil*. San Francisco: Jossey-Bass.

ORNE, M.T. & HOLLAND, C.C. (1968) On the ecological validity of laboratory deceptions. *International Journal of Psychiatry*, 6, 282–293.

ORUM, A.L. (1972) *Black Students in Protest: A Study of the Origins of the Black Student Movement*. Washington, DC: American Sociological Association.

PAPASTAMOU, S. (1979) 'Strategies d'influence minoritaires et majoritaires.' (Unpublished doctoral dissertation. Paris: Ecole des Hautes Etudes en Sciences Sociales.)

PERRIN, S. & SPENCER, C. (1980) The Asch effect – A child of its time? *Bulletin of the British Psychological Society*, 33, 405–407.

PERRIN, S. & SPENCER, C. (1981) Independence or conformity in the Asch experiment as a reflection of cultural and situational factors. *British Journal of Social Psychology*, 20, 205–209.

PRENTICE-DUNN, S. & ROGERS, R.W. (1983) Deindividuation in aggression. In R.G. Geen & E.I. Donnerstein (Eds) *Aggression: Theoretical and Empirical Reviews*, Volume 2. New York: Academic Press.

RAPER, A.F. (1933) *The Tragedy of Lynching*. Chapel Hill, NC: University of North Carolina Press.

REICHER, S.D. (1984) The St. Paul's riot: An explanation of the limits of crowd action in terms of a social identity model. *European Journal of Social Psychology*, 14, 1–21.

RICE, R.W. (1978) Construct validity of the esteem for least preferred coworker (LPC) scale. *Psychological Bulletin*, 85, 1199–1237.

ROSENTHAL, R. & ROSNOW, R.L. (1966) *The Volunteer Subject*. New York: Wiley.

SANTEE, R. & MASLACH, C. (1982) To agree or not to agree: Personal dissent amid social pressure to conform. *Journal of Personality and Social Psychology*, 42, 690–700.

SAYLES, S.M. (1966) Supervisory style and productivity: Reward and theory. *Personnel Psychology*, 19, 275–286.

SCHACHTER, S. (1951) Deviation, rejection and communication. *Journal of Abnormal and Social Psychology*, 46, 190–207.

SEARS, D.O. & McCONAHAY, J.B. (1969) Participation in the Los Angeles riot. *Social Problems*, 17, 3–20.

SEARS, D.O., PEPLAU, L.A. & TAYLOR, S.E. (1991) Social Psychology (7th edition). Englewood Cliffs, NJ: Prentice-Hall.

SHAW, M.E. (1981) *Group Dynamics: The Psychology of Small Group Behaviour*. New York: McGraw-Hill.

SHAW, M.E., ROTHSCHILD, G.H. & STRICKLUND, J.F. (1957) Decision processes in communication nets. *Journal of Abnormal and Social Psychology*, 54, 323–330.

SHELLOW, R. & ROEMER, D.V. (1966) No heaven for 'Hell's Angels'. *Trans-action*, July–August, 12–19.

SHERIDAN, C.L. & KING, R.G. (1972) Obedience to authority with an authentic victim. Proceedings of the 80th Annual Convention, *American Psychological Association, Part 1*, 7, 165–166.

SHERIF, M. (1935) A study of social factors in perception. *Archives of Psychology*, 27, Whole No. 187.

SHERIF, M. (1936) The *Psychology of Social Norms*. New York: Harper & Row.

SHERIF, M., HARVEY, O.J., WHITE, B.J., HOOD, W.R. & SHERIF, C.W. (1961) *Intergroup Conflict and Co-operation: The Robber's Cave Experiment*. Norman, OK: University of Oklahoma Press.

SHIBUTANI, T. (1966) *Improvised News: A Sociological Study of Rumour*. Indianapolis: Bobbs-Merrill Co.

SINGER, J.E., BRUSH, C.A. & LIBLIN, J.C. (1965) Some aspects of deindividuation: Identification and conformity. *Journal of Experimental Social Psychology*, 1, 356–378.

SISTRUNK, F. & McDAVID, J.W. (1971) Sex variable in conforming behaviour. *Journal of Personality and Social Psychology*, 2, 200–207.

SMELSER, N.J. (1963) *Theory of Collective Behaviour*. New York: The Free Press.

SMITH, P.B. (1995) Social influence proceses. In M. Argyle & A.M. Colman (Eds) *Social Psychology*. London: Longman.

SMITH, P.B. & BOND, M.H. (1993) *Social Psychology Across Cultures: Analysis and Perspectives*. Hemel Hempstead: Harvester Wheatsheaf.

SMITH, P.B. & PETERSON, M.F. (1988) *Leadership, Organisations and Culture*. London: Sage.

SORRENTINO, R.M. & FIELD, N. (1986) Emergent leadership over time: The functional value of positive motivation. *Journal of Personality and Social Psychology*, 50, 1091–1099.

SPERLING, H.G. (1946) 'An experimental study of some psychological factors in judgement.' (Master's thesis, New School for Social Research.)

SPROTT, W.J.H. (1958) *Human Groups*. Harmondsworth: Penguin.

STOGDILL, R.M. (1974) *Handbook of Leadership*. New York: Free Press.

TANFORD, S. & PENROD, S. (1984) Social influence model: A formal investigation of research on majority and minority influence proceses. *Psychological Bulletin*, 95, 189–225.

TURNER, J.C. (1991) *Social Influence*. Milton Keynes: Open University Press.

TURNER, R.H. (1964) Collective behaviour. In R.E.L. Faris (Ed.) *Handbook of Modern Sociology*. Chicago: Rand McNally.

TURNER, R.H. & KILLIAN, L.M. (1957) *Collective Behaviour*. Englewood Cliffs, NJ: Prentice-Hall.

TURNER, R.H. & KILLIAN, L.M. (1972) *Collective Behaviour* (revised edition). Englewood Cliffs, NJ: Prentice-Hall.

VAN AVERMAET, E. (1996) Social influence in small groups. In M. Hewstone, W. Stroebe & G.M. Stephenson (Eds) *Introduction to Social Psychology* (2nd edition). Oxford: Blackwell.

VITELLI, R. (1988) The crisis issue reassessed: An empirical analysis. *Basic and Applied Social Psychology*, 9, 301–309.

WATSON, R.J. (1973) Investigation into deindividuation using a cross-cultural survey technique. *Journal of Personality & Social Psychology*, 25, 342–345.

WILDER, D.A. (1977) Perceptions of groups, size of opposition and influence. *Journal of Experimental Social Psychology*, 13, 253–268.

WILLIS, R.H. (1963) Two dimensions of conformity–nonconformity. *Sociometry*, 26, 499–513.

WOOD, W., LUNDGREN, S., OUELLETTE, J.A., BUSCEME, S. & BLACKSTONE, T. (1994) Minority influence: A meta-analytic review of social influence processes. *Psychological Bulletin*, 115, 323–345.

WYER, R.S. (1966) Effects of incentive to perform well, group attraction and group acceptance on conformity in a judgement task. *Journal of Personality and Social Psychology*, 4, 21–27.

YOUNG, K. (1946) *Handbook of Social Psychology*. London: Kegan Paul.

ZIMBARDO, P.G. (1969) The human choice: Individuation, reason, and order versus deindividuation, impluse, and chaos. In W.J. Arnold & D. Levine (Eds) *Nebraska Symposium on Motivation*. Lincoln: University of Nebraska Press.

ZIMBARDO, P.G., BANKS, W.C., CRAIG, H. & JAFFE, D. (1973) A Pirandellian prison: The mind is a formidable jailor. *New York Times Magazine*, 8 April, 38–60.

ZIMBARDO, P.G. & LEIPPE, M. (1991) *The Psychology of Attitude Change and Social Influence*. New York: McGraw-Hill.

ZIMBARDO, P.G. & WEBER, A.L. (1994) *Psychology*. New York: HarperCollins.